PRESCHOOL LEARNING AND TEACHING

PRESCHOOL LEARNING AND TEACHING

CATHERINE LANDRETH
University of California, Berkeley

HARPER & ROW, PUBLISHERS
New York   Evanston   San Francisco   London

PRESCHOOL LEARNING AND TEACHING

Copyright © 1972 by Catherine Landreth.

Standard Book Number: 06-043834-7
Library of Congress Catalog Card Number: 72-86366

CONTENTS

PREFACE

A child begins to learn the day he is born. Starting from scratch, what he learns in his first 5 years is the foundation for all his later learning. What he learns, though, depends on the learning conditions that are his lot. Many persons who do not think of themselves as educators affect these conditions. Who are these persons? Leaving aside his child associates, they are his mother, who is his first and most influential teacher; his father; his preschool teacher and her assistants, aides, and volunteer helpers; or they may be his foster mother or his day care center attendants. All of these persons are deeply and daily involved in creating the learning conditions which help or hinder a young child in what he is most eager to do—to learn—and to make creative use of his mind and muscles. And all of them may at times feel perplexed by portentious pronouncements about the need for understanding "the crucial periods," "the recent revolutions," and "the innovations" in the teaching of young children. Stripped of such mystical terminology as "autotelic responsive environments," the revolutions and innovations are well within the understanding of parents, beginning teachers, and paraprofessionals. This book has, in fact, been written to help beginning teachers and parents make use of what is currently known about the learning and teaching of children between 18 months and 5 or 6 years of age.

To begin with the revolutions, history teaches us that substituting something untried for what has been tried proves, in the main, that there are weaknesses and strengths in both old and new. The fact that something is new does not necessarily mean that it is better, in all ways, than something that is old. What is more, new ideas, innovations if you like, are often old ideas rediscovered and renamed. An autotelic responsive environment, for example, is one that provides enticing and rewarding opportunities for a child to learn and find out for himself what he is ready and eager to learn and find out. Many nursery schools and homes have provided such environments for decades. Comenius, a seventeenth century educator would find little basically new in today's innovations in ways of teaching young children. What would be new to him, aside from attempts to submit speculation, about ways of teaching, to systematic study, would be the use of technology. Talking typewriters were not on hand in the seventeenth century. If you analyze current ways and means of helping young children learn, as I do, in discussing educational strategies, you find that you can sort them out in terms of their emphasis on a child's looking at and listening to a teacher (educational television) or the teacher's looking at and listening to a child (educational play). You also find that educational play materials which induce a child to learn because they present him with an intriguing problem to solve need not necessarily be expensive. With a little imagination in using what is around in the way of materials and experiences, you can help make an infant's or young child's world meaningful to him without using the latest technological devices. One of these devices, a crib which is so wired that an infant by pressing the right button can sound an alarm which brings his mother on the run or can turn on a television program or some recorded music, suggests that use of technology should be tempered by consideration for its possible outcome in producing a push-button civilization. This does not mean that research and experiments in learning and teaching should be disregarded or denigrated. You will find that I draw on research findings to support my suggestions. This book is, in fact, an interweaving of research findings and teaching experience. Because it is a personal interweaving, a few facts about the personal experiences which may have influenced it may explain any biases you detect.

My introduction to school learning and teaching was somewhat unusual. I spent my elementary school years (ages 5 to 12) in a one-room rural school in New Zealand. Two of the 20 children were my brothers. The teacher was my mother. The school had a relaxed family atmosphere in which all the children helped each other and all had some part in teaching as well as learning. This may explain why learning is, for me, something that goes on all the time with no sharp distinction between out-of-school and in-school learning. I also cannot make much of distinctions between work and play. Nor can I separate teaching from learning. If teaching is effective, both teacher and taught learn.

This, at least, was my experience during the 40 years I was involved in some way in teaching young children in college and university nursery schools and in training preschool teachers. During the greater part of these years, I was a staff member of a research institute: the Institute of Human Development in the University of California, Berkeley. While there I was involved both in my own research in early learning and preschool teaching and in guiding the graduate research of the teaching assistants in the nursery school. My working associates were such productive psychologists as Harold and Mary Jones, Jean Macfarlane, Nancy Bayley, Marjorie Honzik, and Erik Erikson. In this research setting all assumptions about learning and teaching had to be tested; all assertions had to be supported by acceptable evidence. This accounts for my references to research findings. The reasons I have not foot-noted each reference are that they represent only a part of the research I drew upon, and I doubt that the scientific journals in which the research is reported would be accessible to most readers. In place of detailed footnoting, I have listed under "For Further Reading" my book *Early Childhood,* which dis-cusses research I mention and can be found in most public libraries.

Recently, while serving as a consultant to the San Fran-cisco Children's Centers, I helped to develop their curriculum guide. In the process, Theresa S. Mahler, director of the Cen-ters, and her staff introduced me to the different worlds of young children in San Francisco's different districts—Chinese, Japa-nese, Italian, Mexican, Black, American Indian, and Samoan. More than this, they showed me how a preschool can relate to its district, by taking into consideration the language or dialect each child speaks and hears at home, the music he listens to, the foods he eats, and the holidays and festivals his family celebrates. This experience accounts, in part, for my emphasis on a teacher's understanding and speaking the mother tongue of each child who speaks and hears a different language at home and on her being able to feel a part of a social group different from the one she grew up in.

Another experience, social rather than professional, occurred when I was director of the University of Chicago Nursery School. I shared an apartment with an anthropologist, Katha-rine Luomala, who was writing up her field work among the Diegueno Indians of Southern California. The field work had included getting information, often in story form, from an informant who was a shaman, or medicine man. Over dinner, Katharine and I tended to talk about what we were doing. During this interchange, it dawned on me that like the shaman, I was describing a kind of subculture, that of a university nursery school: its mores, taboos, and rites. One outcome of my informant role is reflected in my use throughout the book of incidents, drawn from my own experience, which reveal children's and teachers' behavior in different kinds of learning and teaching situations. Another is my basing the training of teachers in having each of them learn to report exactly what she said and did in a particular situation and then try to relate what she did, or might have done, to the outcome of her intervention. This gives a beginning teacher a way of learning from her own experiences and of becoming sensitive to what is going on around her.

The more I thought of the nursery school as a subculture, the more aware I became of the human values it can transmit. This may account for my favoring a broadly based curriculum, rather than exclusive emphasis on "cognitive development." Each child, I think, should be able to find out what he can do, what he likes to do, what he does best, and what is worth doing if he is to get the most he can from his life and give the most he can to the society of which he is a part: the society of man.

Because I am indebted to so many professional associates, as well as to so many young children, for whatever I have come to think about preschool teaching, I cannot make separate acknowledgment to each of them. I must, though, acknowledge the sources of my grandfather stories. They were told to me by Francis Williams, William Norton, and Crawford Somerset. I owe something, too, to Lucile Allen, my long-time nursery school associate who encouraged me during the writing of the book and to Irene M. Vanderpool who not only punctuated and typed my pages but, as a mother of four children, passed judgment on their worth. "Makes sense," she said encouragingly as she handed the lot back to me. And this, I think, is what this book is about. It is an attempt to make sense of preschool learning and teaching and, at the same time, try to make them as absorbing and rewarding as I have found them.

C. L.

PRESCHOOL
LEARNING
AND
TEACHING

1

PRESCHOOL CHILDREN: EACH DIFFERENT

NO CHILD IS THE SAME AS ANY OTHER. OBVIOUS THOUGH THIS sounds, the obvious continues to be overlooked in educational schemes that treat children of the same age as if they should be the same or could be made the same with a bit of "compensatory" education or enforced "integration." As if they were all ready, or should be ready, for school at 5 years of age; all ready or all not ready to read at some arbitrary age anywhere from 2 to 7; and all ready to profit equally from some program or procedure that happens to be the educational rage at the moment.

What makes each child different?

Children inherit different characteristics—among them, learning aptitudes. What a child looks like, how he behaves, and how he learns, is determined in part by the characteristics he inherits from his forebears. The chemical determiners of these inherited characteristics are vast in number and can combine in a vast number of ways, running into several million possibilities. So, unless a child has an identical twin, no other child has his combination of inherited characteristics.

1

What determines the particular combination a child inherits? Chance. And in this chance assortment, some children have better luck than others in their family. Who has ever heard of Michelangelo's brothers?

Children develop at different rates. Children compared with other young animals, like calves or lambs, which walk at birth, take a long time to develop adult behavior. They also develop at different rates. Among babies given fairly equal opportunity to get afoot, some walk at 9 months, others not until 18 months. From what we know at present, it appears as if each child has his own built-in development timer. Giving him unusually favorable opportunities to practice and improve on what he can do may speed up his timer somewhat. By how much or for how long we do not know. What we do know is that a child's rate and stage of development affect how he behaves and what he is able to learn. So, though children the same age are all ready to learn, what they are ready to learn may not be the same for each of them, nor may each learn in the same way.

Girls develop at rates ahead of boys. At the moment of his conception, a child's sex is determined, as well as the inherited characteristics that may help or hinder him throughout his life. Boys and girls not only look different, they behave differently. Some of the differences may be due to parents and teachers expecting boys and girls to be different and giving boys, from birth onward, more freedom than their sisters in boisterous, try-it-out, what-makes-it-tick, stand-up-for-yourself activities. In contrast, sugar-and-spice notions about little girls set most of them gently, but firmly, into habits of docility, compliance, and conformity. Such treatment naturally affects boys' and girls' self-image, their approach to different learning tasks, and their response to different teaching styles. There are, though, some sex differences that appear to be due to differences in the chemistry of boys' and girls' development. As one example, X-ray pictures of children's wrists show the bone development of 6-year-old girls to be a year in advance of 6-year-old boys. This, along with other evidence, suggests that girls mature earlier than boys.

In clinics for children with speech and reading problems, there are many more boys than girls. Why? This sex difference could be due to differences in the frequencies with which boys and girls inherit characteristics that lead to speech and reading problems. It could also be due to differences in their rate of development. It may well be that many boys are not ready for the kinds of learning tasks that most girls are ready for at ages 5 and 6.

Children's environments affect their learning aptitudes and attitudes. All living things are affected by the environment with which they interact. From the moment of conception until birth, a child is in the environment of his mother's womb. What affects her health may affect his development. If her diet is very low in such protein foods as milk, eggs, cheese, meat, fish, and poultry, his brain development may be affected in ways that make him less able to learn. This happens in countries with poor food supplies. It can happen too in rich food-producing countries in which some families either don't know or can't afford the kinds of food they need. Other adverse circumstances that affect a pregnant woman's health may also affect the development of her unborn child: a poor diet may only be the one that occurs most often.

Once a baby is born, he is affected by what feeds his mind as well as by what feed his body. If he has things to look at, listen to, handle, and taste; if he has someone to play with him, listen to him, talk to him, and love him, he makes exhilarating progress in learning; through looking, listening, tasting, touching manipulating, imitating, trying out his instant hunches and practicing and perfecting his emerging skills.

Not all children, though, have so favorable a start in learning. In an orphanage in Lebanon in which babies were kept in sheet-lined cribs all day with nothing to play with, some did not walk until they were 4 years of age. Their sheet-walled confinement did not make it possible for them to learn how to get around.

Even within the same family, each child has a somewhat different environment. A firstborn begins life with younger, less-experienced parents, who usually give the first child more time and attention than their third or fourth. Whatever a baby's birth order, what he looks like and how he acts may also affect his parents' response. An alert, active baby may get more bouncing and baby talk than a passive, placid infant who shows less enthusiasm for adult advances.

Family environments differ too. At the present time, one-tenth or more of families in this country are poorly housed, poorly fed and poorly educated, and have little opportunity to enjoy nature or any of the arts. Though disadvantages of this sort can act as a spur as well as a setback to improving or making the most of any family's environment, a crushing combination of disadvantages can be too much for most families to overcome. Little wonder, then, that a child with a poor prenatal environment, which has marred his development before birth, is likely to suffer continuing handicap because of poor housing, poor health care, poor nutrition, a poor image of himself, and poor opportunities for learning in his own home.

So, since the quality of a child's environment, his inherited characteristics, his sex, and his stage and rate of development affect how he behaves and learns, if you would teach young children, you must *begin where each learner is*. To do this you have to get to know each child and find out what "turns on" each of them to learn. You have also to learn what makes learning take place. Though we still have a lot to learn about learning, what has been learned is worth having in mind.

2
WHAT MAKES THEM LEARN?

WHAT MAKES YOUNG CHILDREN LEARN AS WELL AS GROW AND play? But first, what is learning?

Learning causes and results from chemical and neurological changes in the brain. In laboratories throughout the world, studies are being made of the chemical changes which take place in the brain as a result of learning. Studies are also under way of the changes in nerve cell pathways that have to be made before someone with a brain injury can relearn something like speaking or writing, that he was able to do before the injury occurred. Fascinating though these studies are, they are not much help in making the learning of a particular task like dressing himself, irresistible and inevitable for a young learner. For this we must turn to observations of children learning in a natural setting or to experiments in which children learned well under carefully controlled conditions.

Learning is a from—to process. How do observers and experimenters know learning is taking place? Because there is a *change* in what a child can do or say as a result of whatever training, practice, or experience he is given. This suggests that learning is a from—to process. A 5-year-old boy learning to swim goes *from* being someone who would drown in 5 feet of water *to* someone who can swim ashore and maybe get a certificate for the distance he swam.

Other suggestions that come from studies of learning are that in order for learning to take place, a learner must want something, must pay attention to something, do something, and get something. If to this we add that *he must be ready* for whatever the learning task is, we have some helpful guides in collaborating with infants and young children in what they are most eager to do—to learn.

LEARNING
THROUGH WANTING SOMETHING

What are the wants that incite a learner of any age or species to pay attention and do whatever is required to learn something? Some of the early experimental studies on learning were made on animals. A psychologist found that, by giving a kernel of corn to a hungry pigeon right after it had pecked or poked at a Ping-Pong ball, he was eventually able, by a tireless and timely system of such rewarding, to make a Ping-Pong player of the pigeon. Other experiments on learning in animals, and there are a vast number of them, have been undertaken to find out whether animals learn better; in order to get a reward, like food than to avoid such punishment as an electric shock. This carrot-and-stick approach to learning has long been popular with parents and teachers. Up to now, however, experiments suggest that rewarding a young child for what we want him to learn is more effective than punishing him for what we don't want him to learn.

But, before having done with experiments on nonhuman species, we should note that monkeys and chimpanzees were found to persist for long periods of time in learning to open a puzzle box, simply because they seemed to want to find out how it worked. Their only reward was of a "so that's it" sort.

What do young child learners want?

A young child wants competence. Most of a baby's learning during his first year of life is spurred by his wanting to try out what he can do. He practices endlessly such skills as reaching, grasping, handling, pushing himself along the floor, pulling himself up to a stand, and making a variety of vocal sounds. Even after he can walk and say a few words, his tireless practicing continues. When he can combine two words like "see daddy," he goes on to "see horsie," "see car," or see whatever is around. One child who had 14 two-word combinations of this sort at 2 years of age had 2500 six months later! Another 2 1/2-year-old who was in the habit of talking to himself before he went to sleep had interested parents who put a microphone and tape recorder near his crib. The tapes of his bedtime soliloquies revealed a tremendous amount of self-imposed practice of words and word combinations.

What makes mastery of skills so exhilarating to infants and young children is that they seem to believe that human beings are endowed with magical powers. *And, are they so wrong?* An eager "me do" or "I can do it myself" is a reminder to adults to let a young child do what he is capable of and fairly itching to do—feed himself, set the table, clear away the dishes, mix the paints, or wash the brushes—even if he is at first not as competent as an adult.

A young child wants approval and encouraging interest. A young child is a social creature. He likes to be around folks: not just any folks, but those he knows well—his mother, father, brothers, and sisters. At 6 months of age, he babbles to get their attention, cries when they leave him, and repeats a trick they find entertaining, like yanking off a cloth thrown over his head, clapping his hands, or waving bye-bye. So he learns to do many things solely to please his parents. If, like the Ping-Pong-playing pigeons, he is given a word of praise *right after* he has done something his mother wants him to learn ("Good, you washed your hands before you came to the table," "You put on your shoes all by yourself—let's give you a clap"), he learns to do what his parents praise.

A young child wants to be like an admired person. Much of what a young child learns is through imitating a loved person. A boy becomes a chip off the old block because he tries to be like the father he admires. And because nothing is more flattering than imitation, a father is likely to reward such behavior with affectionate interest and approval. This, though, can create problems in learning. What happens when a 4-year-old boy is spanked by his father for socking his young sister? On the one hand, he is punished for slapping someone smaller than himself; on the other hand, a model of slapping someone smaller than himself is set by the person he loves most and seeks to identify with. What does he learn from this? Probably, to sock his sister when he is out of sight and sound of his father.

What happens, too, when an adult takes a suposedly therapeutic snap at a 3-year-old biter to let him know how it feels to be bitten? What does the biter learn, aside from the fact that he could get a better grip on his companions if his dentition were more advanced?

A young child's survival needs dominate his wants. Though a young child's desire to exercise his ripening skills, to seek adult approval, and to identify with an admired parent are so evident in his behavior, he has, of course, other more pressing physical wants or needs. A child who is hungry, tired, thirsty, cold, or ailing is concerned first and foremost with what relieves his discomfort. Anyone who has heard the outcry of a hungry baby whose feeding hour is overdue knows how difficult it is to take his mind off his most pressing need. So, any preschool child whose basic health needs cannot be adequately met in his home requires supplementary meals and medical and dental care, from whatever source, as an essential part of an effective educational program.

How a young child's wants are met affects what he learns to want. The ways in which a young child's wants are met or not met at home affect the kind of rewards he wants when he enters nursery school and kindergarten. If all a child gets praised and encouraged for is being "good," that is, being silent and inactive and doing what he is told, his desire for competence conflicts with his desire for approval. As a result, he may no longer want what he has had little opportunity to experience—the thrill of achievement. Reviving his desire to explore and enquire and to achieve through his own efforts requires changing what he gets for such efforts. How this can be done is illustrated on page 23. But, before a child can get something he wants through his own efforts, he must first pay attention to something.

What makes him pay attention?

LEARNING THROUGH PAYING ATTENTION
TO SOMETHING

In order to learn, a person of any age must pay attention to something.

Intentional learning is more efficient than incidental learning. Could you, right now, draw a telephone dial correctly? You have probably seen one hundreds of times. If you can't, a quick look at the number and arrangement of holes, letters, and figures should make drawing the dial a simple matter and may convince you that intentional learning is more efficient than incidental learning.

Another illustration of the way in which looking for or

directing attention to something helps learning comes from the training of airplane spotters during World War II. At the beginning of the training program, volunteer spotters could identify four different kinds of planes. After their attention was drawn to wing flow, they were soon able to identify 17 different kinds. One way, then, of directing attention to something is to label it. A host of studies involving young children shows how they can be helped by meaningful appropriate labels.

Labeling marks what is to be paid attention to and learned. In one study, children given practice in throwing rings over a peg were divided into two groups on the basis of their beginning performance being approximately the same. One group was told they would get a star for each ringer they made. The other group was told how to stand and how to throw; when they overthrew, they were reminded, "Too far that time, not so far next throw." The children whose attention was directed by words to what they should do had much better scores than those whose attention was not directed in this way.

Children themselves quickly learn the value of words in directing their attention and activities and so helping them to learn. In an experiment in which children were asked to remember in which box in a row of boxes they saw a piece of candy hidden, they begged the experimenter to put it in the end box. They realized they had a word for the end box but did not have one for a box in another position. A child who has many labels for identifying an object—big or little, round or square, red or blue, half or whole, hard or soft, etc.—has many ways of looking at, thinking about, and remembering an object.

Variety of experience and involvement broadens attention. Another way of directing attention is to give a child several different kinds of experience, all with the same purpose. To illustrate, in a Russian experiment in which toddlers were being helped to learn the names of such objects as a doll, a ball, a toy truck—some children had experience of a "Give me the doll," "You take the doll" sort. Others had much more varied (but no longer) experience of a "Put the doll to sleep," "Lay the doll down," "Lift the doll up," "Rock the doll" kind. Later, when the children were asked to find the doll in a group of objects, those who had more varied experience did better. The variety of their experince had apparently better engaged their attention and made it more possible for them to learn and remember.

This use of a variety of experience in helping a child to learn and understand can also be illustrated by a well-planned nursery school field trip to a fire station. Interest in firemen and fire engines is first stirred by seeing a passing fire engine, with the sirens sounding and all the cars drawing aside to let it pass. At story time, looking at and talking about pictures of a fireman, fire engine, and fire station alerts the children to what they might look for on their trip. After the trip, they hear a story about a fireman, listen to a record ("The Little Fireman and the Big Fireman"), and talk of their own experience. Clapping firemen's hats on their heads and tucking lengths of rubber hose in their belts, they play firemen, sliding down the pole in their tree house and speeding to fires in their wagons. Stacking large blocks, they make a fire station, and in a walk around the block, they look for fire hydrants.

A timely question alerts attention. On a field trip or in the nursery school a teacher's timely, appropriate question may lead a child to notice something he might otherwise overlook. A question involves a child or a person of any age in a way that a statement does not. Consider the apt involving question of a U. S. Customs official at the Canadian border: "Madam, if as you say you have no furs to declare, would you mind my asking if that is your tail hanging down below your coat?"

One of the greatest teachers of all time, Socrates, relied

almost entirely on questions to direct the attention and thinking of his Greek students. Today, "ask, don't tell" might profitably be engraved, at teacher eye level, on the wall of every nursery school and kindergarten.

Contrast, novelty, surprise, and movement grab attention. Visual and auditory attention grabbers have for years been used in advertising. Now they are used in the teaching of young children in the television program "Sesame Street." In this hour-long "show-and-tell" program (the adults show and tell the children), an attempt is made to rivet young children's attention on letters, numbers, colors, shapes, positions, and the appearance and behavior of several animals. This is done through fast-paced changes of content, through somewhat frenzied flashing on and off of letters and figures, through vaudeville jigs and jingles and visual surprises; inanimate objects are animated, muppets speak and sing, and "monsters" unexpectedly crunch their way through letters and words and swallow an unwary announcer.

None of these devices are new. Rhymes have helped generations of children to remember that there are "30 days in September . . . and leap year coming once in four, February then has one day more." The "ABC" song has also, undoubtedly, helped generations to remember the order of the alphabet. As the composers of commercials long ago found out, whatever can be put in words is better remembered in rhyme.

As for visual effects, any contrast alerts attention and could well be used in helping children learn the letters of the alphabet: *o* and *c* or *n* and *m* can be learned as two contrasts rather than as four unrelated letters. Other letters offer similar contrasts that double the return on a child's investment of attention.

Screening out distraction helps focus attention. Another way of focusing attention is through eliminating or reducing dis-

tracting sights and sounds. An adult driving a car on an unfamiliar road has to screen out most of the scenery in order to
keep his eye on the road and the traffic. The ability to screen
out distracting sights and sounds is partly a learned one.
Young children can be helped by having some distractions to
learning screened out for them. So, a well-planned nursery
school playroom is subdivided into activity centers in which
the arrangement of the equipment and furnishing directs the
child's attention to their productive use. In a well-lighted book
center, a bookrack has a table and two or three chairs alongside it. In a carpentry center—usually outdoors so the noise
will be dissipated—the hammer and nails on the sturdy workbench are alongside a bin of wood ends.

Attention-rewarding games encourage focusing attention.
Young children differ in their ability to focus attention and
screen out distracting sights and sounds. They are, therefore,
sometimes helped by attention-rewarding games—a listening
game in which absorbed listening is rewarded with unex-
pected sounds; a feeling game in which concentrated feeling
is rewarded by finding a block or a ball; a stop-and-go game
in which "mice" remain sleeping in breathless suspense until
"an old, gray cat" comes creeping near them.

Most learning tasks involve paying attention to more than
one activity, to doing as well as looking, listening, or saying.
What must a young child *do* in order to learn?

LEARNING THROUGH DOING
AND PLAYING

What a young child does in order to learn depends on the
learning task.

A young child repeats, imitates, and directs his actions. If a
learning task involves coordinating eye, limb, and body movements, as in riding a tricycle, a child repeats or improves on

what he can do or maybe imitates a skillful rider. He may also instruct himself with briefly worded directions, such as "Now I press this foot" and "Now I turn."

A young child explores, manipulates, tries out, compares, and relates. If the task is to find out how something works or is put together, like a picture puzzle, he either *tries it out*—fit or miss—or *figures it out* after looking at and comparing the parts. The younger the child, the more likely he is to try out rather than figure out. The sketch shows a board with a circular groove in which a red, a yellow, and a green peg are fixed and four side alleys. Some adults and young children aged 3 to 6 were asked to move the red peg into the red hole. To do this, the yellow and green pegs had first to be moved into a side alley. Most adults got the red peg into the red hole in 3 moves. The 3-year-olds averaged 36 moves; the 4-year-olds, 25 moves; the 5-year-olds, 21 moves; and the 6-year-olds, 18 moves. The younger the child, then, the more likely he is

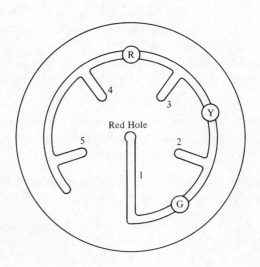

to try out all his instant hunches. This can make him a dangerous experimenter if he does not have an unobtrusive senior collaborator.

A young child figures out, deduces, and induces. When a child is confronted by a problem he cannot solve by experimenting, he draws on his experience to make sense of what he sees and hears.

At a nursery school lunch table, the question of babies' teeth came up. Between mouthfuls of custard, John, aged 3 1/2, asked if babies had teeth. Custard eating was suspended while this problem received the consideration it deserved. Mary, with the conviction born of close observation of a 2-month-old brother, said, "No, babies don't have teeth. Our baby doesn't have teeth." Here, Martha, who has a 9-month-old sister at home, interrupted quickly, "My baby sister Kathleen has teeth." For a minute there was silence while Martha swallowed custard before enlarging on Kathleen's dentition. Four-year-old Dick's eye suddenly lighted, "I know, Martha," he said, "only babies called Kathleen have teeth." Martha beamed, and the entire group returned to the custard completely satisfied with this masterly summing up of the situation.

Actually, Dick had done very well with the information at his disposal, and his teacher made no comment at the time. Unfortunately, for the validity of his conclusion, he had no knowledge of the relationship between age and dentition. The validity of scientists' conclusions is similarly subject to their awareness of the factors involved.

A young child revises his ideas as the result of experience. Two days later, both babies and their mothers visited the group so that the children could see for themselves that babies are not just babies but vary with age in how they look, what they can do, and in the number of their teeth. This led the children to revise their notions about babies and to think and talk about their own and other peoples' ages.

A young child internalizes experiences in mental images or action strategies. A Swiss psychologist, Piaget, offers some helpful speculation on how an infant or young child learns through doing. He suggests that what a young child does becomes part of what he knows because each experience is internalized in the form of a mental image or action strategy. These images or strategies are constantly revised, combined, and rearranged as a child learns from experience.

To illustrate, Piaget noticed that at birth his infant daughter had simple reflex behaviors, such as kicking when lying on her back. As she got older, what began as reflex kicks appeared to be kicks for the fun of kicking. Speculating that she might be able to learn to kick for a purpose as well as for kicks, Piaget put a clear plastic canopy over her crib and laid some light-colored rattles on it. Now kicking produced a jingling sound that the baby seemed to enjoy. To test whether this kicking-jingling experience had changed the baby's kicking strategy, Piaget removed the rattles. Standing at some distance from the crib, he then made a whistling sound the baby listened to. When he stopped, guess what happened? The baby kicked. From this and many similar experiments, Piaget concluded that, in infancy, learning is an interplay between mind and muscle: an ongoing process of adapting or *accommodating*[1] to whatever is slightly different from past experience and then *assimilating*[2] the new strategy that the new experience provides. This calls for storing action images or strategies in the brain in such a way that they can be rearranged and used in a new situation. It also calls for a lot of different kinds of doing, looking, listening, and handling.

[1]Piaget's term.
[2]See footnote 1.

A young child plays. Because most of a young child's doings are of his own devising and because adults rarely see much purpose in such doings, they are referred to as "playing." This raises a question, "Does a child learn through play?" What is play? I have never read or heard an acceptable definition of play, even from its most pasionate promoters. But since there is a general conviction that what young children do is play, look, as I did one morning, at what goes on in a nursery school "free play" period. What are the children doing? And does any part of what they are doing produce a change in doing, saying, knowing, or feeling that could be called learning?

Overflow of activity. Three boys are tearing around the yard, yelling and clutching at each other, tumbling over, tussling, and laughing in an abandon of activity. What are they learning? Maybe that it feels good to abandon yourself to activity after a stretch of quiet sitting or concentrating on cutting and pasting. If this abandon continues, though, it may lead to fighting and crying rather than to channeling energy into something more ongoing and more productive.

Repeating and practicing a skill. In a corner of the yard where there are two swings, a beginning swinger is trying ineffectually to pump herself with an eye on the girl in the other swing who is doing much better. Is the beginning pumper learning anything? She looks as if she could do with some helpful direction or physical assistance in straightening and bending her knees as she goes back and forth.

Copying. A boy has stopped by a painting easel to make a few circular scribbles that he is apparently pleased with and repeats all over the paper. What is he learning? Perhaps to imitate his own circling swoops on the paper. This could be the beginning of learning to copy a letter and thus make a start on early printing or writing, but will it be?

Symbolizing and synthesizing experience. Two boys are attacking a neat stack of hollow blocks, dashing them to the ground and strewing them around. They are so businesslike and purposeful in this activity, I intercede for them when an assistant comes over with a "blocks are for building" gleam in her eye. With the block stack demolished, the boys now set to build with "hard-hat" vigor and assurance. Around this nursery school, no building can be put up until an old one is first knocked down. Though the boys have not said a word about this, they seem to have learned this is so and are expressing it symbolically. *How nearly, though, they missed this opportunity.*

Doing tricks or varying a performance. A boy and girl in the jungle gym are calling, "Teacher, watch me do tricks." They are hanging from the bars by their knees, instead of their hands. What are they learning? To vary inventively what they can do, to plan, and to carry out a plan. This could lead to interest in developing expertise in skills of this sort and give the children more command over and control of their movements. But will it? The teacher merely smiled.

Solving a puzzle that requires form discrimination. In a table pulled out into the sunshine, a girl is putting together a three-part duck puzzle. She has no trouble and is apparently repeating something she has done many times. Will she go *from* fitting a familiar object into its space *to* doing the same with more complex puzzles and finally with symbols, such as *o*, *c*, and *e*? This could alert her to differences in letters as well as forms. Whether it will depends on her teacher and the puzzles provided.

Looking at books. A boy and a girl are each leafing through a book at the book table, showing each other the pictures they like. What are they learning aside from enjoying looking at the books? They *could* be learning to tell the pictured stories to each other and even to recognize an occasional word. But to do this, they might need a little help from a teacher.

As I came home from the nursery school, I passed a school playground where a 6-year-old boy was trying to throw a ball into a basketball ring, with no success. He kept his eye on the ball until it left his hand, and the skewed position of his feet gave a twist to his throw that sent the ball away from the ring. To get the ball into the ring, he will have to learn to keep his eye on the ring, not the ball, and his feet and body faced in the direction he is throwing.

In all the playing I saw, there were *possibilities* for learning. The equipment and materials available—swings, blocks, paints, puzzles, books, and a ball and basketball ring—gave children cues for activity or playing. And there was certainly a variety of activities—repeating, imitating, innovating, comparing, matching, dramatizing, and interacting pleasurably with other children. What specific learnings the activities reflected were not clear *at a glance.* What was clear was that an adult might have added to the learning possibilities in each activity by sensitive intervention into the children's play.

Take the basketball player. An alert teacher could have made a quick check of the ring height and considered ways of making it adjustable: with the ring first at a child's eye height, and then gradually raised. Or she could have asked companionably, "Could I have a throw?" and then mimed a check on her foot placement, a good look at the ring, and with eyes fixed on it, could have made a few preliminary aiming feints before throwing. If after these maneuvers her ball missed the ring, a casual "Too far that time—your turn now," could have paved the way for whatever later developments the child's response suggested.

For such intervention to be effective, an adult has to sense the educational possibilities in a child's activity and, while trying to give it direction and dimension, avoid destroying the child's spontaneous interest and enjoyment or his inventiveness and sense of discovery. Such an adult can help make playing the path to learning. She can also give a playful quality to all learning.

But this brings us to what a child can get from learning.

LEARNING
THROUGH GETTING SOMETHING

What a child gets for what he does may be pleasant or unpleasant or a combination of both, like the carrot-and-stick lot of donkeys.

Getting pleasing results spurs learning to repeat what produced them. When what a child does leads to his getting something that pleases him, his attention, like that of the Ping-Ponging pigeon, is fixed on what he did that produced the pleasant result. He tries to go on doing or learning to do this.

Getting unpleasant results spurs learning to avoid what produced them. If what a child does leads to something unpleasand and frightening, his attention is similarly fixed on what he did to produce his distress, and he tries to avoid doing this in the future.

This sounds simpler than it is. Sometimes a young child is not clear what it is he is being rewarded or punished for. Then, too, what an adult may consider unpleasant or punishing may not seem that way to a young child. If the only attention he ever gets is for "bad behavior," heck, better bad attention than none at all.

If very strong feelings either of pleasure or of distress and fear accompany what a young child does, everything associated with a particular doing may be desired or feared and avoided. If feared, he may literally want no part of it. A 6-month-old baby who has an unpleasant experience in getting shots may become afraid of all men in white coats: butchers, bakers, and barbers, as well as doctors. So what does a pediatrician do? He has an assistant give the shots in another room. And he ingratiates himself with his young patients by having tropical fish, picture books, and playthings in his waiting room, by letting the children handle his stethoscope, by talking with them, and maybe sending them off with a Mickey Mouse balloon.

What a child gets in any experience may thus turn him on or turn him off that experience—and others like it. This turning on, turning off process is called *conditioning* by psychologists. In much the same way as shots may condition a young child against men in starched white coats, his home experiences may condition him to like or dislike what goes on in a good school.

Learning attitudes are conditioned by what children get for learning activities. Take John, a child I know, whose parents are both university professors. From the day he came home from hospital, his parents have rewarded his interest in what goes on around him with interesting things to look at, listen to, handle, put together, and take apart. He has been taken to interesting places—the zoo, the beach, the fire station, and many, many more. His parents talk with him and listen to him, sometimes quote him, read him stories and poetry, and bring him home books from the children's library so he can read his books while they read theirs. In all this, he is not pushed beyond what he can do and seems to want to do. So, he has the self-confidence that comes from success. Now 5, his kindergarten teacher finds him "a joy."

But suppose John had spent his first 5 years as one of five children whose parents were struggling to make ends meet, with neither time nor interesting things (though there are some around) to give their children. No family trips. Very little talk aside from a "stop that—do you hear—." No story reading. No books, though there is a library a few blocks away. No conversation around a table three times a day: instead, irregular snacking with no certainty as to when or what the next meal will be.

Even when their economic circumstances are not downright desperate, many parents turn off their children's urge to know, to do, to say, and to find out for themselves.

I was in Yosemite valley one spring during the Kennedy administration, when there was a great deal of enthusiasm for physical vigor. The valley was filled with sedentary fathers vigorously pedaling around on bicycles, their children following them on wheels of some sort. Other families were toiling up mountain trails with tiny tots held by the hand. As I came down from one of the waterfalls, a young man dashed past, suntanned and in a great hurry, with some shabby snow left over from last year's fall in his arms. He bounded up to a young woman, apparently his wife, with a baby in her arms and a toddler beside her. Dropping on one knee beside the toddler, he said, with the light of revelation in his eyes, "This is snow." And I thought, what a nursery school assistant you would have made. Here you are bringing a phenomenon of nature to share with your little girl. And the little girl did something very typical of children that age. She bent forward and it would have been hard to tell if she were going to bury her face in the snow, smell it, taste it, or feel it. But in that moment *[so pregnant with learning possibilities]* her mother said sharply, "Don't touch it, it's dirty." And I thought, why couldn't you have said, "Feel it dear." And then "dear" would have thought, "This white stuff that dad hurried down the mountain to show me is cold, just like ice cream." And this would have given her a way of thinking about and sorting out the objects in her world—things that were hotter than she was, colder than she was, or just the same temperature.[3]

[3]Catherine Landreth, *Early childhood: behavior and learning* (New York: Knopf, 1967), pp. 270–271.

As for encouraging children to put their thoughts into words, at a meeting in New Zealand of mothers of a rather silent and inarticulate group of 4-year-olds, one of the mothers asked in a tone of incredulity, "Is it true that in the United States children are encouraged to air their views?" But *how can* a child learn he has views if he is never permitted to express them?

Learned attitudes can be changed by changing what children get for learning activities. What can a teacher do to turn on children who come into kindergarten after 5 years of being turned off investigating, putting their thoughts in words, asking questions, speculating, and persisting in order to succeed?

In a nursery school in Tennessee for children who had been turned off from putting their thoughts in words and instead praised for being seen and not heard, speaking is rewarded by making it necessary for children to ask for what they want. These children are eager to use the school tricycles, which are a new experience for them. So, tricycles are kept in a storeroom and brought out only when a child asks for one. At home, these children had been given praise of a hug and "mother loves you type." They are not used to words for something specific they have done, so when a child masters a task, like finishing a puzzle or setting four chairs at a table for four children, his teacher gives him a motherly hug and along with it words of praise, "Good for you, you finished the puzzle all by yourself." Gradually she skips the hug and looks for an answering sparkle in the child's eye for words of praise alone.

Because these children are praised as "good" for being inactive and "no trouble," the teacher rewards doing by giving the child a feeling of getting somewhere. He is praised and encouraged for getting to the top of the jungle gym, where he can look down on her. He is also encouraged and praised in building higher and higher block towers.

This turning a child on to something he has been turned off from is called *reconditioning*. Does it work?

It does!

Here is an illustration: A young child who had been "turned off" barbers and barbering and wanted no part of anything to do with them was "turned on," or reconditioned, *step by step,* patiently and playfully, by his nursery school teacher—Miss L. At a parent's meeting in a nursery school of a small southern college, children's fears were being discussed. One of the mothers reported herself baffled by a fear of the barber shop that her child had recently developed. From the age of 13 months, her son Bud, now 18 months, had been barbered at regular intervals. This he had apparently enjoyed. At 16 months he had been given shots of some kind from the doctor. On his first trip to the barber's after this experience, he cried and struggled as soon as he set foot inside the barber's door. The barber's staff, with more vigor than insight, laid firm hands on him and removed his hair notwithstanding. By his mother's report, this was a difficult experience for all concerned.

On his next trip, his father went with him, taking him to a different barber and planning to have his own hair cut first. The result was lamentable. The child's outcries filled the main street. The operation finished with a frenzied child, a wilted barber, and a father with his hair still uncut.

To bring the matter to a head, the maternal grandmother, who had never seen her grandson, was arriving in four days. Was there any way of removing hair and fear in the interval?

The teacher saw that Bud was not the only member of the family who had undergone a conditioning process. She also knew that his mother was a secretary with limited time at her disposal, so she volunteered to take over the problem.

Having decided that the points of similarity between the two situations were probably white paint, nickel trim, instruments, and a man in a white coat, Miss L. laid her plans accordingly. She first paid a short visit to the barber. Next morning when she and her assistant, Miss W., called for the children in the school car, she had it stop at the post office. She got out and asked Bud to come in with her. He carried in her letters, dropped them in the box, waved to the postman, and got pleasantly back to the car. At school, Miss L. and Miss W. fastened themselves into white uniforms stiff with starch and buttons in place of their customary flowered smocks. Some of the children commented on the change in their appearance, but Bud paid no attention. Ordinarily the very small children (there were three under 2 years) did not use the scissors. This morning, scissors and colored paper were put on the table in their room. While they were playing with these, Miss L. sat down beside them with some paper and dressmaking shears and did a little noisy cutting of her own, rousing as far as could be detected nothing more than mild interest on Bud's part. With the scissors there was a small hand hairclipper, and when Bud and his friend Bill (also 18 months) were turning it over, she showed them how it worked and made a few illustrative snips at Bill's hair. Again, the situation aroused only mild interest.

When the children were playing in the sandbox, she brought out one of their white cotton sheets and asked Bill if he would like her to wrap him up. Bill was a docile child who was willing to stand anything in reason from a well-meaning and presumably kindly adult. Also, he was temporarily sated with sand, so out he came. Miss L. wrapped him with a flourish, smiled, and sat him on a box.

"Look, Miss W.," she said, "here's Bill all wrapped up." Miss W.'s smile and interest acknowledged that wrapping up was an engaging procedure. Miss L. asked Bud if he would like a turn. He came out, was wrapped up, and perched on the box for Miss W.'s inspection. Again, no signs of fear. Bud was unenthusiastic but pleasantly cooperative.

That noon   s the children were taken home, the car stopped outside the barber's shop. Miss L. got out as she had in the morning and asked Bud to come in with her, assuming that they would make a pleasant 2-minute call. Bud put his foot out, looked up, saw where the car had stopped, drew his foot in again, said "No—no," and started to cry.

This was a distinct setback after the smoothness of the morning program; but Miss L. said, with reassuring hopefulness, "All right, tomorrow," and went in to the barber, who said this was just what he had expected. However, he came out to his doorway and, as she got in the car, Miss W. said to Bud, "Wouldn't you like to say 'bye-bye' to the barber?" As the only sort of dealings, social or tonsorial, Bud wanted to have with the barber was to say "bye-bye" and then "bye-bye" rapidly, the car drove off with cordial mutual farewells.

The next day, as the car drove by in the morning, the barber was in his shop window. He waved and the children waved. At noon, going home, the car stopped again. This time Miss L. asked Bill first if he would like to come in with her and then held out her hand for Bud. At the door, his fingers tightened a little; so she lifted him up, judging that the situation viewed from an altitude of 5 feet 6 inches might look a little more acceptable than it had from his original 2 feet 6 inches. Inside the door he gave one look at the barber, clutched Miss L. tightly around the neck, and said "Bye-bye." The barber and Miss L., however, stood their ground.

He said it was a nice day. She remarked on his large wall clock, and moved a little nearer to it. Bud had a distinct weakness for clockwork. "Your clock says ticktock" she said to the barber. He said, yes, he'd noticed that too. They exchanged laudatory remarks about the excellence of his mirrors and chairs and again Miss L. suggested that Bud say "bye-bye." He revived immediately, and they left the shop to a chorus of "bye-byes."

The next day was the third day and a school holiday. Bud's grandmother was to arrive the following morning. Miss L. and Miss W. called first for Bill, who was on the most cordial terms with the barber, and then for Bud.

This time they crossed the doorway without incident. The barber was busy shaving a man in the window and paid no attention to them. In the chair next to the shaving operation was Bud's paternal uncle, almost completely screened by the morning newspaper. As Miss L. surmised then and learned later, he was on hand so that if worse came to worst, the hair would be removed if not the fear.

His presence was a reminder that, though inside, Bud still had quite a way to go. Miss L. sat down in one of the chairs and said, "Miss W., this chair turns around!" and turned once for her benefit. Miss W. said "What a nice ride you're having. Wouldn't Bill like one too?" Bill climbed up and he and Miss L. revolved before Miss W.'s appreciative gaze.

Miss L. suggested that Miss W. would also like a ride, and she admitted that she had been craving such an opportunity. As she seated herself, she suggested that of course Bud would want a ride too and helped him up onto her knee.

As they were successfully completing the second revolution, the barber came over. He had been watching their technique and said, "My chairs ride up and down too." While Miss W. and Miss L. registered appropriate appreciation for the versatility of his furnishings, he deftly raised and lowered the chair, adjusted it to working height, and then reached for his cloth. "Let me," said Miss L., and, smiling at Bud, told him she was going to wrap him up. Miss W. suggested that if he turned around on her knee, he would be able to watch himself in her pocketbook mirror.

From then on, the haircutting proceeded smoothly and pleasantly and without interruption save from the paternal uncle, who came out of ambush to advise that Bill, in undertaking an exploratory survey of the barber's cabinet, was "fixing" to drink some of his hair tonic. Bill was immediately "unfixed," and the now sleek-headed Bud returned to his home, with a suggestion that his mother have him call casually at the barber's sometime before his next haircut.

You may feel that Miss L. spent more time than most adults would be willing to devote to such an enterprise. Actually, what was done was all a part, and merely a modification, of the procedure in a child's nursery school day. That a little time and thought spent this way are a saving in long-time wear and tear is indicated by another experience of Miss L.'s.

Some years later, while in a hairdressing cubicle, she heard a child's screams, which followed a recurring pattern of mounting crescendo to a sharp shriek followed by sobbing diminuendo. The attendant explained, "You'd never guess," she said, "There's a small boy out there having his hair cut. His father is holding him in his arms and walking around the room. The barber is creeping up on them from behind taking a quick snip between screams. Isn't that something?"

It was—something that could have been handled better.

For children older than Bud who are turned off learning rather than barbering, here are some ways a teacher can make achieving rewarding.

The thrill of achieving can become a substitute for instant material rewards. Because things may mean much to a child who does not have many things of his own, a child can be given a string of 10 beads of different colors to take home and keep when he knows the colors and can count to 10. Let him "tell" his beads at home. When he can do a hard puzzle, let him borrow it overnight to show the home folks what he can do. When he has a favorite story he can tell as he leafs through a book, let him borrow it to tell to a little brother or sister. When cookies are made at school as part of learning to measure and count, a cookie for each member of the family, counted out, can be taken home in a plastic bag. When seeds are planted in small painted tins, why not let each child take home the one he has tended for Mother's Day?

Since children take home pictures made with school paper and paints and boats made with school wood and nails, why not some of the other things they do or make? The cost is small, and the return can be large.

A child's learning progress can be made evident to him. For a child to feel he is learning, he needs to see for himself that he can do something today he could not do yesterday or yesterweek. A friend of mine had a young grandson drop in on him on his way home from a New Zealand infant school. "Well, what did you learn today?" grandad asked. "Nothing, we just developed," said the 5-year-old, fresh and unimpressed from what his teacher had called a "development period."

So, to help a child interested in letters see that he is "getting his letters," give him a sturdy manila envelope to hold each letter he knows printed large on a 3-by-4-inch card. He can then see that he is progressing from a 2-letter to a 12- or 26-letter learner. When he recognizes a word or two, help him start his own dictionary: a card for each word he knows held together with a ring through a hole in each card.

What a young child wants, pays attention to, does, and gets depends on his maturity and experience: on what he is ready for. How do we know what a young child is ready for?

LEARNING THROUGH BEING READY
TO LEARN

Several years ago a psychologist interested in finding out whether maturity or training was more important in a young child's learning to ride a tricycle, roller skate, swim, and climb planks, gave one member of a pair of twin boys training in each of these performances at the earliest age at which his behavior suggested he might be ready to profit from such training. Though she began training him to ride a tricycle at 11 months, it was not until he was 19 months old that he made any progress. He was apparently not ready to learn this skill at 11 months but *was ready* at 19 months. By then, he had the nerve muscle coordination necessary for beginning to ride a tricycle.

Other evidence of the effect of readiness or maturity on what a young child can learn and understand comes from the Swiss psychologist Piaget. He noticed that, up until 6 months of age, a baby reaching for a ball lying in front of him withdrew his hand and gave up all reaching activity if a cloth were laid over the ball. At this early age, out of sight was literally out of mind. The baby was not ready to look for something he had seen hidden or to understand that it still existed even if he could not see it. He was like Baby Nell in the nursery rhyme:

> *Baby Nell has 10 little toes.*
> *Baby Nell has 2 little hose.*
> *She always stares when her hose go on,*
> *As though she thinks her toes have gone.*

Not until 8 months of age did Piaget's baby lift the cloth and look for the ball he had just seen covered.

What is involved in both the 8-month-old infant's and the 19-month-old-boy's being able to learn something they had not been able to learn earlier is a maturing of brain functioning and of the nerve muscle coordination that the brain controls.

Preparatory experiences help ready a child for learning tasks. Time is not the only factor in attaining maturity and readiness.

And nowhere is this better illustrated than in the way a baby learns to look at, reach for, grasp, and manipulate objects. Detailed analyses of this kind of learning in babies from 3 to 6 months of age show a learning progression that can be briefly sketched in words that suggest the influence of experience:

A 3-month-old baby lying on his back has his gaze directed to his hands because they are waving in front of him. A bow tied to each wrist makes hand-gazing even more intent.

As he looks, by chance his hands touch each other. Now he both sees and feels their touching, and this links nerve cell pathways in his brain.

As this touching experience is repeated and enjoyed, he tries to repeat it himself. Working a 12-hour day, he becomes able, with time and practice, to bring his hand movements under control of his eyes and will.

This prereaching progress continues when he becomes able to bring his hands from outside his field of vision toward something he wants to reach.

And so, looking, reaching, grasping, and manipulating develop through a ripening, readying process that requires both time and "playing with his hands."

Is there anything adults can do to help a baby get the kind of experiences he is ready for? But, how do we know what he is ready for?

A child is ready to learn slightly harder, slightly different tasks from those he has already mastered. When a baby shows by his shifting gaze that his eyes can follow a moving object (first days of life), he is ready for a gently moving mobile hung up where he can see it or for an adult's nodding head or smiling face.

When his gaze rests on a face bent over him (first month),

he is ready for things to look at of interesting color and shape hung up where he can see them.

When he swats at what is within reach (from 3 months on), he is ready for something to swat—dangling balls or bells from a bar over his bed that reward him with jingling sounds.

When he can grasp, as well as reach, he is ready for things to grasp with different feels—slippery, plushy, hard, soft.

When he starts *putting* things into something (pegs in a can) and taking them out, he is ready to try *fitting* them in (pegboards).

When he can fit pieces into the spaces they fit, he is ready to pay attention to shape—first familiar objects, then abstract forms, then symbols presented in form board sets that contrast their shapes—such as *o*, *c*, and *e*.

At each stage, he is eager to learn—to find out what he can do, to practice, and to try what is just *a little harder* and *a little different* from what he has already mastered.

A young child has an urge to practice his ripening skills. How do we know a young child is eager to learn? Because all investigators of infant behavior note infants' urges to practice their ripening skills. The reason a toddler is always on the go is that he has just found out he can go.

Recently I was making an afternoon call on a new university faculty family. There were two other callers. As the ladies sat comfortably slumped in overstuffed chairs, the 15-month-old son was brought in from his nap. He had just started walking a few days earlier and, now refreshed by sleep, was eager to get afoot in the large living room with its thick pile carpet. He was happily lurching from chair to chair with an occasional clutch at the furniture when tea was brought in. Then he was briskly picked up and popped into a 3-by-4-foot playpen. A kitchen strainer was dropped in alongside him. The boy, apparently a child of spirit, flung the strainer into the room and literally howled with rage. "Got a temper," said one of the childless callers. What this child had was a legitimate grievance. A large space admirably suited to the safe development of upright locomotion was being monopolized by four middle-aged ladies, none of whom showed any intention of more virogous activity than stirring her tea. If the persons present had to be divided into those confined and those free, clearly a developmentally informed justice would have reversed their positions.[4]

What a young learner wants to do is, thus, what he feels ready and eager to master and what is just a little different from what he can do already. Part of a teacher's task then, is to *match* what a child *can* do to what he *could* do in learning about his world and his relationship to it.

[4]Catherine Landreth, *The psychology of early childhood* (New York: Knopf, 1958), p. 117.

3

WHAT CAN THEY LEARN?

THE YOUNG CHILD IS LIKE THE RENAISSANCE MAN   He is interested in whatever comes within his ken; and he usually wants to know, do, or say right away. This is what gives an early learning curriculum its whatever–whenever, anything–anytime quality. It cannot be presented to a young child in prepackaged subject-matter chunks at prearranged times. Nor is a child always learning what an adult thinks he is learning. An aunt took her 6-year-old nephew to a children's symphony concert in an opera house. The boy sat in rapt absorption throughout the first number, his head back, his gaze aloft. When the number ended and his aunt was congratulating herself on the musical pleasure she was giving, he asked matter of factly, "How do they change the lights in the ceiling?" Apparently he had been pondering the mechanics of changing light bulbs at a height of several stories. For all his aunt knew, he had been barely conscious of the music.

How can a teacher sharpen her awareness of the learning possibilities in children's interests and activities? One way is to keep in mind the *basic sensory motor skills, thinking proc-*

esses, concepts, and speech forms a child has to master in order to process the information he gets from his senses and, thereby, get some understanding of his world. This, though, is not all a teacher needs to have in mind. Besides knowing what a child at a particular level of development could learn, she needs to know what she could do to help promote the learning. She has then to find whether the child *is* learning what she is trying to promote. This is not easy.

A teacher seldom has as convincing and immediate evidence of the effectiveness of her teaching as an English grandfather I know. He had picked up his two grandsons, aged 4 and 6, at their school and was driving them home. Preoccupied with his thoughts, he was aroused by the boys' noisy scuffle over possession of a book. "You should try to effect a compromise," he said in grandfatherly tones. "Compromise, grandad," said both boys, arrested in midassault by a new word with crunch to it, what's that?" What granddad said, I do not know. Judge for yourself how effective it was from the outcome. Two days later he was driving the 6-year-old to school on one of those English mornings, when the BBC announces that there will be intermittent sunshine. The grandson was silent, looking pensively out at the low billows of clouds occasionally parted by a gleam of sun. "Granddad," he said, "the sun and the clouds are trying to effect a compromise." The BBC could not have said better.

Because a curriculum for early learning is so free and wide, listing learning sequences in different activities and areas of interest can help give it structure and direction. And, suggesting teaching devices to promote these learning sequences and assessing devices to find out what is learned may help make the curriculum credible and usable. This is what I will try to do in some from–to progressions in 17 related areas of early learning.

The order of their presentation is based on the relationship between the areas. A young child's activity usually involves learning in several areas simultaneously.

FROM-TO PROGRESSIONS IN SEVENTEEN RELATED AREAS OF EARLY LEARNING

FROM SENSING TO SORTING AND SYMBOLIZING

A baby is a glutton for sensory experience. Even in the first days of life, he turns his eyes and head in the direction of a moving light. Sudden sounds cause changes in his activity and heart rate. And, when different patterns of checkerboards and parallel lines are hung up where he can see them, the length of time he looks at each suggests that he prefers some patterns to others and is beginning to sort them out. Early on, anything put into his hands is brought to his mouth for tasting and testing. And when he can both reach and grasp, he makes tireless use of that first research tool, a pair of hands, to feel and manipulate whatever comes within reach.

All this sensing leads to sorting out his impressions. Sensing and sorting pave the way for use of symbols: for spoken and, later, written words. Nowhere is the relationship between sensation and symbolization more clear than in Ann Sullivan's teaching her blind and deaf pupil, Helen Keller, the word for water. She pumped water into one of Helen's hands while spelling, in touch symbols, the word for water into the other hand. Once Helen grasped the relationship between sensations and symbols, she was quickly able to enlarge her vocabulary.

So it is with the young child who sees and hears. To get the sense of words, he has to have the sense experience for which the words are symbols. As he looks, listens, feels, smells, tastes, and handles, he gets the sensory experiences that make meaningful and necessary such words as light and dark, hard and soft, heavy and light, silky and scratchy, hot and cold, steady and wobbly, sweet and sour, big and little, loud and soft, red and yellow, square and round. Many 2-year-olds whose homes provide free access to a variety of materials and to the time and attention of an adult who tries to make life interesting and meaningful for them have this kind of experience. There are, though, both 2- and 3-year-olds who have not had sensation and symbolization related in this way. So a nursery school or day care teacher needs to help each child progress from his present level of experience in sensing and symbolizing, regardless of his age. How is this done?

Provide materials which offer a variety of sensory experiences. Water in a tub or pail with things to wash, plastic cups and jars to pour or sprinkle from and into, and bubble pipes offer fairly dry water experience indoors if there are waterproof aprons for each child. Outdoors, a watering can, a sprinkler, a wading pool, a drinking fountain, and 4-inch paintbrushes and small pails for water painting yard equipment are possibilities for providing various sensory experiences with water.

Sand, wet and dry, in sandboxes or sandtrays, with pans for pies; spoons and scoops for tunnels; sieves for sifting; and some hard-rubber small trucks and cars for sand roadways offer a wealth of experience with sand.

Clay or play dough can be kneaded or pounded on a washable surface. Rolling pins, cutters, and tongue depressors can be used to flatten, divide, stretch, and dent.

Crayons, chalks, and finger paints combine color and texture experiences.

Blocks of different sizes and shapes make size and shape a matter of feeling as well as seeing.

A feeling box or bag in which objects are placed for feeling what is soft, what is hard, what is round like a ball, or square like a block, is more interesting when what is felt can be compared with duplicate objects in a clear plastic bag.

A xylophone in a part of the room removed from quieter activities gives a child a chance to listen to sounds of different pitch. So do tuned bells or water glasses.

Pictures and picture books offer two-dimensional representations of familiar three-dimensional objects. Children need some experience with pictures before they can accept them as representations.

Accept a range of acceptable use of materials. Provided a child's use of materials does no damage to property or persons, the freer he is, the more likely he is to learn what he is ready for. All that he needs to know is that water stays in the tub and sand in the sandbox. Clay is for kneading; paste for pasting, not eating; and pictures are for looking at, not scribbling over. Within these limits, one child may use dough or clay as something to feel and touch, another may treat it as a medium to make a snake, a man, or whatever.

Associate symbolizing with sensing. Just as Ann Sullivan associated the word *water* with its splash into Helen Keller's hand, so a teacher can associate words with sense experiences. "What a *high* tower you are building." "That block feels a little *wobbly*." "The clay seems a little *hard* today." "What does sandpaper feel like?"

Provide materials for sorting, matching, and identifying.

SORTING ACTIVITIES In a home or nursery school in which there is any kind of orderly use and storage of materials, a child sees a great deal of sorting in terms of use. Clothes are put away in cupboards or drawers, books are on shelves or bookracks, perishable food is in the refrigerator. In the nursery school, blocks of different sizes go back on shelves that have pasted outlines of the size of block they store. When a child has finished his first course at lunch, he puts his plate on the pile of plates on the clearing-away table, his fork and spoon on one tray, and his glass on another. Sorting objects on the basis of size, shape, or pattern is thus not an unfamiliar process. A game can be made of sorting by using a treasure box full of buttons of different colors and sizes, spools of different sizes, beads of different colors and sizes, pieces of material of different colors and textures, and stray bolts and nuts. The ones that are the same can be put together in plastic jars. Berries, leaves, or nuts of different sizes or shapes can be sorted in the same way. When a child can sort on the basis of one characteristic, such as color, his next step is to sort on the basis of two—big red or small white beads or buttons.

MATCHING AND IDENTIFYING ACTIVITIES Form boards and puzzles require a child to look carefully at picture parts or geometric shapes to see which shape and size of piece fits into the space where it belongs. Lotto games call for matching a picture held up by the teacher with one of four pictures on a large card.

IDENTIFYING ACTIVITIES In lotto games, for example, a teacher can ask a child if he can find the picture of a train or tricycle on a card of four pictures.

Provide guidance in the use of matching materials. Since puzzles, form boards, and Montessori equipment pose a matching problem, their value lies in their being used in the way they were intended. Young children who have no experience in their homes with educational play materials need some example, assistance, and encouragement in using form board, puzzle, or lotto-type materials. For this reason, it is necessary to have several sets of each form board or puzzle so that a teacher can sit down with four or five children who all work together, each on a similar problem. Once a child sees the purpose of the material and is successful in its use, he can be free to make his own choice and work alone.

Provide a range of difficulty in matching forms. Once a child can make a three-piece duck puzzle and has had a chance to make it often enough to savor his success and gain confidence, he may be tempted to try something harder—a four-piece dog or a five-piece train puzzle. As children get better at putting together pieces of a familiar object, they often like to turn the puzzle upside down to see if they can make them without the picture. When a child shows he is ready to move from familiar objects to abstract or geometric forms, the next step in progression is to match symbols—letters. A puzzle that shows some contrast in the shapes of letter insets, such as *o*, *c*, and *e*, alerts a child to the differences between these three letters. So does a puzzle with *i*, *l*, and *t* insets or one with *u*, *w*, and *y*.

Name printed letters and words. Many young children are eager to know letters and words. They realize that some squiggles mean something to adults and older children. So, as a child recognizes *o*, *e*, and *c* by name and appearance, why not give him an envelope with the letters he knows? And encourage his interest in finding the letters he knows on buses, labels, and name tags. To encourage him in decoding and encoding, once he has three letters that can be combined in a word of interest to him, such as dog or cat, let him begin his own dictionary—a card for each word he can recognize held together with a snap ring.

Because so much of a young child's sensing and symbolizing is associated with manipulation and movement, his sensory development cannot be separated from his motor development. Here, too, his learning reflects a progression; not so much in symbolizing as in control and coordination.

FROM SPONTANEOUS TO CONTROLLED, COORDINATED, SELF-DIRECTED, AND IMITATIVE MOVEMENT

The motor behavior of young children has its beginnings in the early weeks of prenatal life, a fact we are artfully reminded of by the title of a research report—"Fetal Frolics." Nursery school children are still frolicsome. A yard full of young children is a yard in motion. If we look more closely, though, we can see great differences in the children's activities and skills. Some are graceful and fluid in movement; some awkward and jerky; some lumber around; others dart here and there like hummingbirds; some perform with virtuosity on horizontal bars, trapezes, ladders, and knotted ropes; others have no tricks at all. Indoors, some children of 3 are copying letters and drawing recognizable houses, men, and airplanes; others don't draw at all and, when pressed in a test situation, can't copy a circle, cross, or square. At 3, some children can hold up their right hand when asked; others are floored by this request at 5. Here and there a child stands out because his activity has a restless, driving quality—he can't hold still—while all that another child does looks like a study in slow motion—he can't get going. What is the significance of these characteristics? What do they mean in the life and learning of a child?

Mastery of motor skills enhances a child's self-image, gives him confidence, and is an asset in his playing with other children. Listen to the pride with which he calls, "Watch me do tricks." Control, coordination and self-direction of movement are necessary for almost any task he sets himself, from unscrewing a knob to printing his name. Also necessary is the ability to inhibit movement, to stay put, and to sit still long enough to find out what is happening.

As a child moves in different directions—up the ladder, down the slide, through the barrel, and around the sandbox—he gets a sense of direction and location in space that makes position words meaningful to him. He literally tests prepositions in his muscles. And because adults are so right and left in their use of eye, ear, hand, and foot and in reading and following traffic directions, a young child has to get some feeling of right and left in order to make sense of much that he sees and hears. He has, too, to learn to copy movements. This helps him to copy the movements made with a pencil on paper in printing letters and words. So, there are more outcomes from large-muscle activity of young children than the fun it gives them (not that the fun should be devalued).

What can a teacher do to encourage young children's enjoyment of a variety of activities and their progressive development of control, coordination, self-direction, and imitation of movement patterns?

Provide opportunities, lacking in most homes, for a variety of motor activities.

RUNNING Children need clear open space and a ground surface that does not graze their knees if they fall. They enjoy handballs and footballs to run after, wagons to pull, and planks raised from the ground at one end to give a running start.

THROWING Beanbags, being easy to grasp, offer a good first experience; balls call for more skill. A hoop or box to throw the balls in calls for still more skill and precision in throwing.

JUMPING A bouncing board made of an 8-inch flexible plank, supported at each end, and about 5 inches from the ground, gives children a chance to bounce up and down and acquire the motion and spring necessary for jumping. So does a trampoline. A jumping pit with a sawdust or tanbark bottom makes for easy landings.

CLIMBING   Stairs have interest for the youngest children. The junior-size jungle gym (or some equivalent), with its many bars and footholds, offers increasingly difficult problems in climbing, as do two rubber tires suspended by a rope ladder or a commando net hanging from a tree house.

PEDALING   Kiddie cars for the younger children; tricycles for the older ones; and a smooth, level, or slightly sloping paved space to ride them on furnish various degrees of pedaling experience.

PUSHING AND PULLING   Hollow blocks, wagons, planks, ladders, and spades for digging invite pushing-and-pulling activities.

HITTING AND PUNCHING   A punching bag and two pairs of boxing gloves help eye, hand, and foot coordination.

SUPPORTING OWN WEIGHT   A horizontal bar and parallel bars offer opportunities for bar-circling and "skinning the cat."

KICKING   A football, and the space to kick it in, and a punching bag suspended by a long string at comfortable kicking height promote eye and foot coordination.

CREEPING AND CRAWLING   These activities are encouraged by having casks the children can crawl through, boxes with small openings to squirm through, and inclined planks. In one nursery school, the children have had great pleasure from crawling through sewer mains discarded from a factory.

RHYTHMIC EXPERIENCES   Good equipment for providing rhythmic experiences are a seesaw that is firmly fastened at the pivot and has handles at each end for the children to grip; a bouncing board; rocking boats of various types; a swing with a canvas or leather seat (a wooden seat may chip front teeth), a trapeze, rings, and a trampoline.

HAMMERING, POUNDING, AND CONSTRUCTION Wooden pegboard for the younger children, and hammer and nails, lumber, screws, hooks, glue for the older ones make pounding and construction irresistible.

SWIMMING Given a mild climate, a satisfactory swimming pool, and a teacher who can make swimming fun for young children, most children can learn to swim before 5 years of age. and thereby add to their pleasure and safety around a pool.

Provide for degrees of skill as well as variety. A wooden ladder firmly lashed at one end to the jungle gym may offer a daring climb for a novice, a rope ladder free at one end may be needed to challenge a veteran climber. When a child starts throwing a ball over the fence, this is the cue that he has tired of merely throwing it into the air and is ready to aim it somewhere. This is the moment to bring out a basket, pail, box, or anything into which he can throw his ball and thus progress from throwing to aiming. When children begin to run their wagons or tricycles into equipment or walls, this is the moment to develop an obstacle course. Children can then progress from bumping to avoiding and to more skillful steering.

Make motor activity safe. Aside from providing a soft landing under all climbing equipment, making activity safe is largely a matter of supervision and slogans. Effective supervision means enough staff coverage of activity areas. As for slogans, the following are examples of some cautionary comments:

JUNGLE GYM

"Two hands to climb."

"Hold tight."

"Catch the plank by the cleats."
"Catch the ladder under the bars."
"Watch for fingers."

BOUNCING BOARD AND SPRINGBOARD
"One at a time."

TRICYCLES AND WAGONS
"Good drivers look out for people."

ROCKING BOAT
"Wait till the boat stops to get off."
"Both hands on the rail" (for small children).

SLIDE
"Off the slide Bill, John's coming down." (For the younger children, one-way traffic is encouraged.)

HAMMERING AND POUNDING
"Hammers and saws stay at the bench." (Unless a child has a specific legitimate purpose, hammers are used only at the carpenter's bench.)

Dangerous activity should of course be redirected, and any child pushing another on a high place should be immediately grounded until he can remember to play safely at a height. Safe use of equipment can be approved with a "nice driving" to a child who steers his tricycle out of the way of another child running in front of him. The captain who stops his passengers from rocking a rocking boat until the last child gets on can be commended with, "John is a good captain—he waits till all the passengers are aboard."

Make motor activity attractive. Because motor activity is attractive to most children, it hardly needs pushing, though an occasional child may be helped by a teacher's supporting presence and words of encouragement as he climbs up a ladder. Children from age 3 on are seldom "in character" in their motor activity, so provide simple props to help them support their roles: hats for firemen, truck drivers, and construction workers; lengths of hose for service-station attendants; and chains or ropes for trailer towers.

Children also get fresh ideas for activity if occasional changes are made in the positions of the movable equipment in the yard. In Berkeley, two blocks with a plank ramp leading to and from the blocks was immediately called the "Bay Bridge" and invited pedestrian and truck traffic and toll collection.

Plan activities and games that help children inhibit movement. Being able to sit still or stay put long enough to pay attention to what is being done is harder for some children than others. Such children can be helped to cope with their restlessness by blowoff activities: punching a punching bag, wrestling a tackle dummy, or even taking a brisk run around the yard. They are also helped by a program that alternates sitting still with activity periods and that can be flexibly adjusted to a particular child's needs on a particular morning.

Listening games or dramatic games that call for inaction, such as "The old gray cat comes creeping, while the little mice are sleeping," or rhythmic activities that require the children to stop marching or running when the music stops help to make a game of what is hard for them.

Associate position and direction words with children's movements. There are many opportunities to associate words and movements like those below:

up	under	in	far	from
down	before	out	farther	in front of
on	behind	near	next to	round and round
over	between	nearer	to	

Introduce movement-imitation games. In the first year of life, babies learn to imitate movements. They clap hands for daddy, they wave bye-bye, and they patty-cake. Though these may seem a far call from learning to imitate or copy a move-ment pattern like a circle, a letter, or a figure drawn on a piece of paper, they represent an early stage in learning to write.

At a later stage, around 3 or 4 years of age, children enjoy imitative singing games, such as

"Did you ever see a lassie go this way and that?"
"I put my right hand in, I put my right hand out."
"Open them, shut them."
"An eency weency spider came down the waterspout."
"Simon says put your hands on your head."

Provide materials for copying activities. For decades, copying has been virtually banned from nursery school activities, so great has been the devotion to freeing the child's creative impulses. In view of the relationships established between children's ability to copy a circle, triangle, square, or diamond and their readiness for reading and writing, perhaps this has been carried too far. Some simple pegboard or beadboard designs that can be copied and some letters that can be traced or copied at least give some clue to each child's level of sensory motor coordination. If such materials are placed in a separate unit away from the art activities, they need not shackle children's creative impulses, particularly if copying is done on ruled paper with kindergarten pencils rather than on unruled paper with crayons, as is true of the art activities.

Provide materials for small-muscle coordination. Even in the first year of life, babies concentrate on picking up pieces of fluff or small crumbs with finger-and-thumb precision. By 2 or 3 years of age, they are ready to button, snap, zip, hook, and buckle, if these activities are made attractive by having Montessori frames for buttoning and lacing to work on or a doll that can be dressed or undressed only by zipping, snap-ping, buttoning, hooking, and buckling.

Materials like Krazy Ike's, puppets, pegboards, or puzzles

all call for some precision and delicacy in manipulation. So do miniature animals, dolls, doll tea sets, spoons, and skillets. The harder the activity and the more concentration it requires, the more inviting it should be. I remember some years ago seeing a cerebral palsied child learn to control his tongue muscle by poking his tongue in and out. His teacher held a Lifesaver on a stick in front of his mouth so that each time he poked his tongue out, he got a lime lick. The same child was helped to focus his eyes on a moving object by watching an electric train run around a circular track on a table, making a cheerful toot each time it passed the station.

Just as it is difficult to separate motor from sensory development, so also is it difficult to separate motor from language development. Speaking is *a motor activity*. Infant vocalizing and chanting is *an accompaniment of activity*, and words later become *a substitute for gestures and actions*. Still later, silent speech *is used to direct activity*.

FROM BABBLING
TO LANGUAGE

—*as communication*
—*as a means of structuring thinking and feeling*
—*as an art medium*

A child's speech has its beginning in his first months of life in his selective interest in speech sounds. The speech he hears affects the number and kind of speech sounds he makes himself. Infants in institutions or in homes where they hear little speech babble less and make fewer speech sounds than infants who are spoken and listened to. So, by the time children reach nursery school, they have had very different experiences in the language samples they have heard and in the encouragement they have been given to speak for themselves.

A teacher's first task, then, is to encourage each child to have confidence and trust in his ability to communicate with whatever language he has. Speech, though, has a wider purpose than communicating instant needs or feelings and responding to adult imperatives of a "do" or "don't do" sort. To think well, a child has to speak well. So, he has much to learn: not just words for objects, but words for their characteristics, so he can sort them out as big or little, few or many, red or blue, square or round, heavy or light; and as being in, on, under, over, or wherever. He has also to learn how to pluralize in a language in which there are many irregularities and how to take the shortcuts pronouns offer in referring to property ownership. He has to speak of the past, the ongoing, and the future, as well as the present. And because most happenings are not invariable and absolute, he needs words to express how much and how often—"always," "sometimes," or "usually." To relate happenings to their cause and consequences, he needs "because" and "if . . . then. . . ." To suggest alternative possibilities, he needs "or" in his vocabulary. And he has to master the English sentence, with all the information it can give about who did what to whom and the clues it offers to the kind of word that comes next.

He can learn, too, how to use words to evoke feeling. A 3-year-old in the backseat of a convertible said, "The wind is washing my hair." And he can get a sense of rhythm and rhyme in the way he puts words together. Some 3-year-olds have made a good start on all of this. Others have barely begun.

How can a teacher help learners at such different levels?

Developing confidence
in verbal communication

Try to assess each child's language development. In the home visit that precedes a child's nursery school entry, a teacher gets some idea of how a child is spoken to and in what language or dialect; what books he sees; and what stories he is read, if any, and the use of television and radio. She can also see whether he is encouraged to use words or actions to get what he wants.

Communicate with the child at his level. For a child with little speech who communicates with a hug or pat, return the hug or pat; but add a few words ("Hello Mary, you are the first one here") and gradually skip the hug and bring a sparkle to a child's eye with words alone. For a child who speaks a foreign language, a teacher needs at least a basic vocabulary in his language. To teach him the standard English she uses, she must *understand and respect the language he uses.*

Suggest words to take the place of action. To a child tugging on another or trying to snatch something from him, say "Tell him what you want; maybe he will give it to you."

Contrive situations that require a silent child to ask for what he wants. When a child comes up to a teacher, takes her hand, points or looks in the direction of something he wants, try, "Tell me what you want, Bill," and repeat after him, "You want the hammer?"

Telephone to a reluctant speaker. Telephoning (by toy telephone) restricts communication to the spoken word and gives a child the opportunity to imitate an adult activity.

Introduce identification songs. To a small circle of backward speakers, sing, "Good morning little yellow bird, good morning little yellow bird, who are you?" while looking at a child in a yellow sweater. He is then encouraged to sing back, "I am Billy Bunting, I am Billy Bunting. That's my name." The group can then chorus, "He is Billy Bunting, that's his name." Or sing, "Where is Lucy, where is Lucy?" To which she responds, "Here I am, here I am, I am Lucy." Chorus, "There she is, there she is, there is Lucy."

Expanding vocabulary
for objects and their characteristics

Give children experiences that make words meaningful. During World War II, a 3-year-old boy whose mother dropped him at the nursery school on her way to an assembly-line job at a ship-building plant, was greeted by a child who snarled at him with clawed fingers, "I'm a tiger." The son of the tin-hatted, overalled mother roared back, "I'm a sembly line." Clearly, he had little idea of how his mother spent her working hours.

Without leaving nursery school, many of the day's experiences can be drawn on—for example, the names of fruits and vegetables, their colors, and how they were cooked by simply asking, "What vegetables today? Which ones did we have yesterday?" Picture books can be leafed through with a "Show me the truck," "What's this?" or "What else flies?" Miniature transportation toys can be held up or picked out of the feeling bag and named; red chips can be sorted from blue ones. All this helps a child learn characteristic and class names as well as object names.

Make up a word-guessing game. Say "I am thinking of something red—something in this room," or "I'm thinking of a vegetable . . . no, it's not a green vegetable . . . it's an orange one."

Make up stories about characteristics of objects and activities. What is hard, what is easy, or what is slow can become a story illustrated by pictures cut out from magazines.

Developing clear articulation

A child who articulates well is more likely to be listened and spoken to than one who does not speak clearly. He gets more practice, encouragement, and pleasure from speaking. So, poor articulators need help—but not harassment.

Set a good speech model. Two-year olds in particular are helped by having the teacher look at them, bend down to their level, and speak slowly and distinctly, using short, simple sentences.

Repeat a child's unclear words without criticism. To a child who says "wabbit," say "Yes, the rabbit is hungry." To the child who says "tink," add "I think so, too."

Encourage but do not coerce a poor articulator to join in jingles and finger plays. Many jingles, finger plays, and nursery rhymes with taxing consonants at the beginning, end, or middle of words are listed in the Oxford Dictionary of Nursery Rhymes. Try "Hey diddle diddle," "Peter, Peter, pumpkin eater," "Hickory Dickory Dock," and "Humpty Dumpty."

Replay a tape of a child's speech. Listening to his own speech can help a child compare how he sounds with how he thinks he sounds.

Using plurals, pronouns,
and sentences

"Oats, peas, beans, and barley grow" suggests the use that can be made of food count and mass nouns at the lunch table. During dressing, *foot* and *feet* come easily into conversation. Miniature models of men, boys, girls, animals, sheep, and dogs, and picture books with a single animal on one page and several on the facing page invite the use of singular and plural forms.

Relate pronouns to the persons' names for which they substitute. Me and *mine* come early in a child's speech, though adults often perpetuate the use of a child's own name to refer to his belongings. Everyday use of "Give that to John—it's his" or "Would you give that to me—it's mine" give a child a fair sample of pronoun usage. Because nursery school property is shared, some care has to be taken in referring to, "*your* turn on *the* tricycle" (not "your tricycle").

Use sentences in speaking. A young child's first speech has a telegraphic quality: "See ball—that block." Such telegraphic statements can be expanded by the teacher's adding, after a child's, "That a ball?" "Yes, that is a ball" or "That is a block." Or something can be said about each of them. "The ball is red" or "The block is heavy." When a child responds to a query of "Who brought this to school?" with "Bill," say, "Yes, Bill brought it to school."

Use questions to draw attention to sentence parts. "Who did?" "What did he do?" and "What did he do it to?" can be followed by a summarizing sentence that illustrates the convenience of the sentence form. But don't be stuffy about it.

Pause in a story or verse for children to complete a sentence. Children get to know their favorite stories and verses word for word. Repeating or completing sentences from memory gives them sentence practice.

> *Way down south where bananas grow,*
> *A grasshopper stepped on an elephant's toe.*
> *The elephant said with tears in its eyes,*
> *"Pick on someone your own size."*

Introduce transformations from positive to negative. When animals are brought to nursery school, children often compare what one can do with what another can. So, it is easy to introduce "Fish swim." "Do birds swim?" "No, birds don't swim." "Do rabbits swim?" "Do fish fly? "Do fish creep?"

Test a child's ability to anticipate a word from the context. "Soup is hot, ice cream is ———." "A dog barks, a cat ———."

Ask a child to deliver a message for you in a sentence. If the child does not deliver the message in sentence form, a staff member can help the child reconstruct it by the questions she asks.

Using tense and mood

Without some grasp of the use of past, present, and future tenses and active and passive moods, a child cannot communicate effectively or handle relevant facts.

Contrast today's events with yesterday's and tomorrow's. "What did I read yesterday?" can be asked at story time. And if there is no time to read a story that the children ask for, "I will read it tomorrow" gives a model for future reference. There are many occasions on which a teacher can recall yesterdays and anticipate tomorrows. Stories help, too: After Goldilocks' visit to the bears' house, Little Bear says, "Someone's *been sleeping* in my bed and *here she is.*"

Using words that qualify, compare, relate, and express frequency and cause

How often something happens is as important as the happening. There are many occasions on which *always* or *sometimes* can be introduced: "What do we *always* have for lunch?" "What do we *always* do before we have lunch?" or "*Sometimes* mothers come to see us."

Give reasons for rules, such as, "We won't play outside today *because* it's raining. *If* it stops, *then* we can go out."

Give children experience with comparatives. Ask questions about which is the bigger of two blocks or the biggest of three or which is bigger, an elephant or a cat. Help children to think in comparative terms: "Which is *faster*, a car or a tricycle?"

Telling a story

As children listen to stories, read or told, they get a model for telling about happenings or experiences in the sequence of their occurrence. When you pause after "And then what happened?" children get a chance to interject part of the action into an ongoing sequence.

Tape children's stories. When a child has something he would like to tell you or tell the children, suggest that he could tape it and then hear it played back to him. Or, you could write it down and then read it back to him just the way he said it.

Invite children's collaboration on a story of what they did. Children like to hear stories about what they did. In making a story of some field trip or special occasion, a teacher can pause for their prompting.

Encourage children to tell picture-book stories as they turn the pages. Because picture books for young children have a "cinematic" format, the stories can be told from the pictures; this is one way of introducing children to reading.

Expressing what is felt and imagined

What a child feels and imagines is as much a part of his life and world as what he sees and does. So, his fantasies and make-believes should be accepted in an "I, too, make-believe" spirit. Some of the children's fantasies are violent and destructive—so, too, are adult fantasies in folktales. In the books, stories, and verses read to children, fantasy, as well as fact, should be represented. The sound as well as the meaning of words should be considered in choosing a story.

A child who learns to love books and stories often wants to "read" them for himself. His wanting to read is a natural outcome both of this love and of his interest in decoding letters and words. So, several young children literally teach themselves to read in the same way they teach themselves to speak. Most, though, need considerable help in this undertaking. Some ways of giving this help are suggested in the following section.

FROM DECODING GRAPHIC SYMBOLS
TO READING

No early learning activity arouses more controversy or more conflicting claims for its merits than learning to read. What does a mother mean when she says her 5-year-old can "read"? Does she mean he knows the letters of the alphabet? That he recognizes a few printed words like his name and the name of his favorite cereal? That he can read a particular primer? That he understands what he reads? That he reads aloud, slowly and mechanically, or silently, with instant comprehension? And what pleasure or profit does he get from whatever he reads?

What is reading? Reading is a complex process in which several component skills must be mastered. It requires, first, that a reader be able to distinguish between graphic symbols, such as *o* and *c*. He must also know the sound each represents. This calls for putting together or integrating what is seen and heard. The reader must then be able to see a page of print, not as separate symbols, but as ever larger symbol chunks— first words, then sentences, and then paragraphs. To do this he must follow, with eye and mind, the left–right direction in which letters are combined into words and words into sentences. For a young child who points to pictured objects on a page in a random here-and-there order, this left–right direction has to be learned. Moreover, since written words stand for spoken words, if they are to have meaning for a young reader, he must have a good vocabulary. He must also have sufficient grasp of sentence structure and rules of grammar to be able to anticipate what kind of word comes next in a sentence. Then, too, his immediate memory must be good enough for him to connect the sentence he has just read with the one he is reading in order to keep some thread of meaning. All of this requires interest, concentration, and the ability to sit still, as well as some breadth of experience and some maturity of the central nervous system. So, any question of when a child is ready to learn to read can be answered only in terms of his readiness for one or more of the component reading skills.

When is a child ready to learn to read? A child who speaks well and understands what is said to him; who is interested in conversation, books, and stories; who sits absorbed with a picture book, telling stories from the pictures; who can finish almost any sentence in a favorite story and can recite some nursery rhymes has the kind of language development and interests that make some attempt at reading almost irresistible. If in addition he is curious about letters, knows the letters of the alphabet, and finds them in traffic signs and automobile licenses; knows a few words and asks what a word on a billboard says, he is showing many signs of being ready to teach himself to read. These, though, are not the only signs a child gives of readying himself for some of the skills involved in reading.

What are signs of getting ready to decode graphic symbols? As early as the first month of life, infants in laboratory experiments look longer at some patterns of lines than others when the patterns are hung up where they can see them. This suggests that they distinguish one from another and are entering a preparatory stage for later decoding of graphic symbols.

At 15 months, a child, given some demonstration and encouragement, pats the bunny pictured in that charming baby book *Pat the Bunny.* His recognition of a drawing as a representation of a familiar object becomes even clearer when, around 18 months, he points to the correct picture in answer to "Show me the baby" or "Show me the ball." Still later, he can answer correctly when asked "What's this?" as his mother points to a picture of a ball or a kitty. These are signs that he is ready to associate a spoken word with a pictured representation of an object: a step on the way to associating a spoken with a written word for an object.

Other readying performances are sorting and matching objects of different shapes and putting the pieces of a puzzle into the space they fit. These reflect a child's recognition of likeness and difference in the shapes and outlines of objects. If the puzzles he fits together involve putting lowercase letters in the spaces they fit, he is readying himself for distinguishing between the letters of the alphabet.

Noticing what is missing in an incomplete drawing (a rabbit with one ear) and knowing such directions as up and down, around and across, left and right are further signs that a child has cues for distinguishing between *o* and *c*, *b* and *p*, and *b* and *d*. Being able to arrange in order a Sequee, which is a set of four pictures showing a left-to-right sequence of action or to read a pictograph recipe reflects a start in the left-to-right reading of symbols.

No one of these skills is "reading," but each helps to ready a child for decoding letters into sounds and written into spoken words.

What are readying experiences for enjoying and using books?
Five centuries ago, few people could read and there were few books in circulation. Stories and information of various sorts were communicated through spoken words and pictures. A very young child is also preliterate. He, though, sees books, magazines, and newspapers and people reading them. The more he sees of this and the more he is read to, the more interested he is likely to be in reading. When he leafs through a book *as if* he were reading it, making up his own story about the pictures, he shows that he is ready to get ideas and enjoyment from books and is aware that they are "read" in some way. When he begins to watch the print as well as the pictures while he is read to and completes a sentence when an adult pauses, he is again readying himself to associate the written with the spoken word, even if he still relies heavily on the pictures for meaning. When he can tell you the words in

his picture dictionary, chances are that here, too, he is making some association between the printed and the spoken word. In all these experiences his interest is whetted for reading, just as it was for speaking by hearing people speak and realizing that every object around him had a name. In learning to speak, though, a young child is not given formal instruction. He picks up his mother tongue from what he hears. In contrast, his learning to read is considered a task requiring formal instruction, with heated controversy over which method or system is best, and often with remarkably poor results.

Is there one best method for learning to read? Among the methods of formal instruction in reading are the "look say," which emphasizes visual recognition of words; the phonics method which emphasizes learning the sound of words and their spelling; and the International Teaching Alphabet method, which uses a symbol for every vowel and consonant sound in the alphabet—thereby sparing a child *until later* from learning that a letter can have more than one sound, depending on what letters come after it. There is also a linguistic method, which introduces children to words like *ran, can* and *man* before *cane* and *mane,* in which the *a* sound is changed by the *e* that follows. And there is a color method, in which children are given clues to the pronunciation of vowels and consonants by their color. There are, too, different approaches to reading aloud—in a group, in a pair, or individual sessions with a teacher. And there are a variety of reading kits and beginning readers that emphasize some variant of the different methods of instruction.

To test these methods, there is an ongoing national research project sponsored by the U.S. Office of Education. There are also volumes of research literature on the outcomes of teaching different groups of children by different methods. And there are volumes of research literature on remedial reading programs to help a child who has had the wrong method at the wrong age *for him*. As a result of these efforts, there is fairly general agreement that no one method is best for all children and that the method has to be adapted to the child rather than the child to the method. There is also fairly general agreement that not all children can or should learn to read at the same age; that boys are more likely to have difficulty in early reading than girls; and that both boys' and girls' interest in reading is affected by what they read about. So, the younger the child, the wiser it is to let him proceed at his own pace, giving him experiences that may interest him in teaching himself to read and giving him whatever help he seeks—in short, making reading attractive and *elective*. This approach does not deprive the ready and eager to read. Nor does it frustrate the uninterested and unready who may profit much more from some other type of educational experience.

What can be done to help a child raring to read? What can be done to make decoding fun?

Give a child an envelope with a lettered card for each letter he knows. A young child often asks what a letter is or wants to print on his paintings the first letter of his name. Why not give him each letter he knows printed on a card to keep in his own envelope? Once a child has enough letters to combine in a word, he is ready for some words without having to wait until he has learned all the letters of the alphabet.

Provide letter puzzles with slotted three-dimensional letters. Letter models that a child can run his fingers around help him get the feel of a letter; so does fitting the letter into its slot. Because children enjoy puzzles, alphabet puzzles with three or four letters to a puzzle, such as *o, c,* and *e* or *i, l,* and *t* can help to acquaint children with the letters of the alphabet.

Devise letter-matching games. Here is a letter-matching game devised by one of the teachers in the San Francisco Children's

Centers. Note the teacher's provision of simple materials, her use of encouragement and questions, the children's awareness of their learning goal and their progress, and the game spirit.

To some 4-year-olds looking at the wooden alphabet letters and turning them over, the teacher said, "Would you like to play a letter game with me?" "We play it with cards," she explained as she made room for four players around the table. Dealing from a stacked deck of 2-by-2 cards in runs of five of the letters *o, c, e, b, p,* she dealt one of each, face up, to each child and face down to herself. "What's that letter?" she asked as she dealt each one. "How did you know?" With children's attention alerted to differences between a line that goes or doesn't go all the way around, to a line across, a line up, and a line down, she explained, "This game is to see if you can find the letter *l* turn up in your letters. When you find it you can turn yours down." She held up *o,* which three of the players found at once and eagerly helped their slower fourth player to find. "Good," said the teacher. "One down. How many still up?" "Now find this one," and she proceeded from *c* to *p,* each time encouraging children's comments on how they found the letter and asking how many down and how many still up to generate interest in getting all five cards down.

By the time the five cards were down, child watchers were asking for a "turn," but the "players" were eager to repeat their success in a second round. At the ·end of this one the teacher told them they could make the letters they had played with, if they would like to try, using the ruled paper and pencils on the shelf. Next time they played, she added, there would be some different letters. Since letter-matching interest continued high, the teacher made some 6-by-6-cardboard sheets, each with four letters which could be covered by 2-by-2-matching letter cards in an accompanying box of letters and used by a child working alone at his own pace.

Over several days the children gradually learned to match all 26 letters, to name them, and to recognize them in their own printed first name. Progressing to words was a logical next step.[1]

Devise letter sound games. Asking children what words they know that begin with a *ku* sound, like cat, corner, and coke, paves the way for relating letters to words.

---

[1]San Francisco Unified School District, "Alphabet game," *A curriculum guide for children's centers and prekindergartens* (1969), pp. 9–10.

Help children make traffic signs for truck and tricycle traffic. Many children know *stop* and *go*. Those that don't can become more familiar with these words by using traffic signs in traffic play.

Label what children use. Labels suggest the usefulness of printed words when each child's locker has his name on it, when shelves are labeled, and when cans of poster paint have a strip of the paint color with the label (red, blue, yellow, or whatever) printed in white.

Devise label games. Putting word labels where they belong can be an interesting game for children who are interested in reading labels.

Provide flannel-backed alphabet letters and a flannel board. For the child who knows one or two words, "making" his words offers both challenge and achievement.

Start a dictionary for each child with each word he knows printed on a separate card. Most nursery school bookracks have a picture dictionary. In the early stages of recognizing printed words, a child can see his progress in the number of words in *his own* dictionary.

Illustrate the stories you tell with a flannel board. Illustrating a story with picture cutouts in a left-to-right order gives children a preliminary experience with the left-to-right direction in reading. So does arranging a set of Sequees and reading a pictograph recipe.

The only point to decoding graphic symbols is for the information, interest, and pleasure the decoded words give. So what can be done to make decoding worth the effort?

Make books and stories a source of delight. Provide a rack of books for children to look at. When a variety of books are always available, children have more opportunity to look at them, point to the pictures, and talk about them. They get some feeling of reading the books even if they are not actually reading the printed words.

Make up stories about the children's doings. A teacher-composed story with some contributions from the children suggests how they too can compose stories.

Encouraging them to tape or dictate their own stories has already been discussed on page 55.

Provide taped readings of the storybooks on children's shelves. When children can both see and hear the words of a story, not only does the relationship between spoken and written words become clearer, but almost immediately, some children begin to recognize some of the written words.

Reading cannot be separated from writing and spelling. So, the kinds of materials and activities that encourage writing and spelling also encourage reading.

FROM SCRIBBLING TO WRITING

Making a letter in the sand with a stick, in the air with a finger, or on paper with a crayon or pencil helps a child to remember what a letter looks like. Writing is, though, a time-consuming, laborious operation for a young child and requires fine muscle coordination, of which he is incapable. So, the only point of writing in the first 5 years of a child's life is to help him understand and use graphic symbols, *if this is something he seems very interested in doing.* What can a teacher do to help a child who either has or might develop this interest?

Let children scribble. Given paper and sturdy crayons, what a young child does first is scribble on it. If he is free to do as he pleases, provided he confines his scribbling to the paper, he tends to copy his lines and circles in repetitive scribbling. Since writing requires copying movement patterns made by someone else, copying his own movement patterns is a first step in this process.

Assist and encourage name signing. The letters a young child is usually interested in making are the letters of his name. He sees his name on his locker; he wants his name on the picture he paints. So, when a child asks to have his name printed by the teacher, why not show him how to make the first letter? Then he can see and hear that *B* is the first letter for Bill, Bob, and Ben. Something more is needed to mark his painting. His teacher can suggest that he make the first letter and she will make the other ones until he learns how to do this.

Provide printed name models. One way of helping a child is to give him a model of his name to copy, as well as a demonstration.

Provide a name or letter stencil. Another way of helping a child is to provide a name or letter stencil. This helps to give him the feel of making letters and ensures instant success and the confidence this brings.

Direct attention to the capitalized first letter in a child's name. A young child's interest in writing his name provides a natural introduction to the two kinds of letters, lowercase and capital, and to the use of a capital letter in beginning a person's name.

Utilize occasions that require and reward name signing. Valentine Day and Christmas are natural occasions for having the children exchange cards and thus use their name-printing skill. If a child cannot print his name or can only print one letter, the teacher can help him to print what he cannot.

Introduce mechanical means of printing. We live in an age of printed and typed rather than handwritten words. Children can at least get some notion that there is more than one way of getting a letter or a word onto a piece of paper if an old typewriter on which they can do some supervised experimenting and some letter and word stamps they can use freely are provided.

Provide ruled paper and a kindergarten pencil for printing. To make a distinction between free drawing and attempts at writing or copying letter, provide ruled rather than plain paper and a pencil rather than a crayon for writing.

FROM EXPERIENCING
TO PROCESSING INFORMATION

What a young child experiences depends on how he "processes" the information he gets from each experience. What is processing information?

A mother of a 5- and a 9-year-old daughter was spending a night alone with her children while her husband was out of town on a business trip. In the week before his departure, there had been two burglar alarms in the neighborhood. These had not been mentioned in front of the children, and the mother was not unduly apprehensive until she was aroused from sleep by a noise in the dining room downstairs. Looking down the stairway, she could see light under the dining room door and hear soft closing of drawers and a muffled clink of silver being moved. Now, wide awake, she aroused the 9-year-old and told her to tiptoe down with her and stand ready at the front door to make a dash for the neighbors on command. Thus supported, the mother flung open the dining room door with a forceful, "What's going on in here?" only to find the 5-year-old carefully setting the table for breakfast. "What in the world are you doing?" the mother asked. The little girl looked quite crestfallen. "I wanted you to think the fairies had done it," she said.

How was a 5-year-old to know that soft sounds of silver being lifted in the middle of the night would be processed by a mother as a project for the police rather than an undertaking of the fairies?[2]

[2]Catherine Landreth, *The psychology of early childhood* (New York: Knopf, 1958), p. 242.

How could she know that what a mother thinks is affected by experiences of which a 5-year-old may have no knowledge?

A young child, too, processes what he sees, hears, and feels by relating it to what he has already seen and heard and has a name for.

Two-year-old Tina, visiting me with her father, went out on my patio to explore. She returned almost immediately, saying, "wee-daw, wee-daw." She seemed excited by some discovery she wanted to share. I looked at her father for interpretation. "She is saying, "Wee door," he said as we went out with her. In the patio below, with its low fence to contain the neighbor's puppy, was a small picket gate. Tina had spent her first 2 years in a house set in a wide-open space. She, therefore, did not know that what swings on hinges outdoors is called a gate. She had, though, done very well in classifying a new object by relating it to what she already knew and had a name for.

Processing by classifying

Comparing what is seen with what has been seen and recognizing what is the same and what is different is a beginning in classifying objects and actions in ways that make them easier to think about. For classification to be helpful, though, a child has to see for himself that any object or action can be classified in many different ways. An apple is round in shape, red or green in color, big or little in size, and is a kind of fruit that may be encountered ripe or unripe, raw or cooked.

What can a teacher do to expand a child's experience in classifying?

Listen to the ways each child classifies. What a child thinks is the same or different gives clues to what he thinks important as well as to experiences he lacks. It also gives some clue to whether he takes time to observe and compare. One child who was shown pictures of a black-spotted Dalmatian dog, a black-spotted banana, and a French poodle and asked which pictures were the same, took a quick glance and put his fingers on the banana and the Dalmatian dog. At that point, a few questions—"Why do you think these two are the same?" "Could you tell me what this one is?"—pointing to each of the three pictures with no criticism in word or tone, might have led to reflection.

Devise some classification games. Sets of miniature vegetables and fruits can be used in a game in which a child sorts out all the things to eat, then all the fruits and all the vegetables.

In another game, buttons of different sizes and colors can be sorted as big and small, red and yellow, big red and big yellow, and small red and small yellow. Or a teacher can hold up a big red button and have the three or four children playing with her find one to put alongside hers. Some of the best sorting experiences are the ones a child embarks on for himself in playing with miniature animals, Noah's Ark sets, and Matchbox trucks and cars.

Plan experiences in which one material is used many ways. A store of smooth pebbles gathered from a beach can be used for counting, for weighing, for water drainage in the bottom of a flowerpot, for making a tin rattle, for decorating a cement block, and for seeing what happens when a pebble and a cork are dropped in a glass of water. Besides having many possible uses, a pebble may be the *last* in a pile, the *only* pebble on the beach, or one of *many*.

Being able to think about an object in more than one way opens up new possibilities for a person of any age in solving problems. In a test given at a university to entering science students, each was confronted by a 3-foot length of narrow metal tubing firmly fastened to the floor. A golf ball lay at the bottom of the tube. On a bench beside the nearby sink were various rods and a rusty can. The test was to get the ball out. Only some of the students saw the solution as pouring water into the tube and thereby floating the ball out.

Processing by quantifying: numbering and counting

Quantification of what is seen early becomes important for a young child. His one nose, two arms, two legs, and the four legs on a dog, a chair, and a table invite comparison in more precise terms than *one* and *many*. And the nursery rhymes and songs he sings, like, "Ba-ba black sheep," introduce names for *how many*. If, though, *number* is to be helpful to a child in processing information, he has to distinguish between number as an *order* in counting—three comes after two and before four—and number as a *total* of whatever is counted. He has also to discover that four pennies or four cookies are still four, regardless of how they are grouped: two and two, three and one, or all four in a row. Number becomes more meaningful, too, when a child discovers number combinations, such as one and one make two, two and two make four, and if one is taken away from four, three are left.

To help understanding number *as an order, provide materials that invite seriating.* Arranging objects in a big-to-small, what-comes-next order is a step toward counting. The pyramid of colored disks given so many toddlers challenges them to put the disks over the peg in the big-to-small order that makes a pyramid. More varied possibilities for experiment are offered by a set of 10 rods ranging in length from 1 to 10 inches, each inch marked by a line around the rod. At the end of each rod is a figure representing its length. The rods invite seriating in stair form.

Introduce counting rhymes and jingles. The nursery rhymes, "One, two, buckle my shoe" or "This old man, he plays one, he plays nicknack on his thumb," give children experience with the order in which numbers come, even though this "eena, meena, mina, mo" approach gives little idea of number as a totality.

To help understanding number as a totality, provide a variety of experiences in counting totals. With the decimal system built into his fingers and toes, a young child is handily in touch with counting material. Variety helps, though, and there are endless possibilities during a day for counting: how many chairs, glasses, and napkins in setting the table; how many paintbrushes for each easel; and how many cookies so everyone can have one. Good counting opportunities in a nursery school are, though, often overlooked.

Recently, I visited one in which a 4-year-old boy was having a birthday party. The "party" consisted of cupcakes and lemonade and an each to his own rendering of "Happy Birthday to You." Not a word about the fourness of four. Why, I thought, couldn't they give the boy four hearty cheers or four loud claps, and why not have him blow out four candles and wear a four on his chest to show that what had been three was now four. Those cupcakes, too, could have had all patterned variants of four decorations, raisins, or whatever. Moreover, since four marked 4 years, why not four pictures on the bulletin board of the boy at 1, 2, 3, and 4 to show that the units counted were large units in development and time?[3]

There is, as this birthday party shows, more to numerical quantity than miserly counting of how many. A child has to learn that four is four is four, no matter what the four objects are or how they are arranged or spread around. Here, again, a teacher can help him.

Provide number-grouping materials and activities. If a child is to get the idea that four chips are still four, regardless of whether they are arranged in a line, square, or triangle with

[3]Catherine Landreth, *Early childhood: behavior and learning* (New York: Knopf, 1967), p. 238.

a spare chip to one side, he has to have a lot of experience in handling, matching, and sorting four objects arranged in different ways. Buttons sewn on cards or dots arranged on cards in different groupings are obvious possibilities for matching and sorting. So are some pegboard playthings that require a child to match the number and arrangement of holes in a disk with the number and arrangement of pegs on a pegboard over which each disk fits. Activity possibilities are endless. As one suggestion, a child can add four stars or spangles to a collage in whatever pattern he chooses.

Provide materials and activities that associate numbers with numerals. In matching and sorting, associating *how many* with its numeral is a help, particularly for a child who already recognizes some graphic symbols and who may have a picture book that shows a numeral alongside a collection of dogs, cats, or whatever.

For a child who plays with dominoes and can match dot groupings and who also has some experience with rolling dice and counting how many peanuts or bottle caps his throw entitles him to, it is but a step forward to match *4* with four peanuts or four bottle caps. Nor is it taxing for a teacher to devise endless matching and sorting activities that require putting all possible groupings of three, four, or five dots alongside *3, 4,* or *5.* A helpful device is "Numberites," a series of 10 cards with both the numeral and the grouping of dots on each one. Each card also has the same number of notches as dots on one side, which fit into the same number of gaps in the card that is next in the number series. Where each card fits is where it belongs in numerical order.

Provide materials that help a child discover number combinations. From number groupings, it is only a step to number combinations: to seeing that two is one and one; that four is two and two, three and one, and four ones. The series of 10 rods already referred to is useful in helping children discover such number combinations. When several sets of these are available, a child can hardly help noticing that he can combine two or three short rods to make one the same length as a longer one—he may even notice the rods' numbers and see that a two-and-two combination makes four.

All this counting *how many* by numbers prepares a child for measuring *how much*, also in numbers.

Processing by quantifying in units of measurement

Today's child lives in a world in which we seek more and more exact measurement of more conditions. Much of our understanding is in terms of numbers rather than words. A child hears the radio and TV weather announcer report the day's temperature as a number of degrees, the rainfall as a number of inches, and the wind force as a number of miles an hour. If his height and weight are measured in the nursery school, he has some experience with linear and weight measurement. If he is a front-seat driver and sees his father checking the speedometer, he is at least exposed to the measurement of speed, and if his parents are keen photographers who carry around a light meter, he is aware of the measurement of light. As he helps his mother pick up quart and pint cartons in the supermarket and hears her order 5 gallons of gas at the service station, the measurement of volume also becomes a part of his experience. Exposure of this sort may not, however, mean much to him because he is not actually involved in the measuring process.

One spring when chickens were hatched in a nursery school and children measured their height on an inch ruler and their weight on a kitchen scale, they were asked next day what they had measured. "A chicken," they all said. A child has to have many firsthand experiences in measuring length, height, weight, volume, and temperature before he understands that he is measuring a characteristic of an object rather than the object itself.

Provide a variety of measuring instruments and opportunities. Cooking necessitates measuring volume, time, and temperature, and a building project leads to linear measurement. When children were making a playhouse in a nursery school yard, they first walked off how big they wanted the floor to be and then measured it with an architect's steel measuring tape before going to a lumberyard to get 2-by-4's and planks cut to the length they needed. Raising chicks for a week creates an opportunity for using an inch ruler and kitchen scales to see if each chick is getting bigger and heavier. Once a child has had some supervised use of measuring instruments, he can have them available for his own appropriate use. A simple balance, some weights, two plastic measuring cups, and jars of pebbles, absorbent cotton, sawdust, and plastic packing curls invite ongoing measurment of weight in store play.

Processing by relating parts to wholes

In daily living, a child sees one cookie serve two children when it is halved. He sees an unwrapped loaf of bread fall into 10 slices, each a part of the loaf. Part–whole relationships thus become a part of his experience and can lead to understanding simple fractions. A quarter of an apple cut for each child at the end of the midday meal can clean teeth and at the same time, give visual experience with halves and quarters.

Processing by inferring causes and predicting consequences

Children's enjoyment of a nursery song, "Oh Dear, What Can the Matter Be," reminds us that young children ponder causes of a "how-come" sort and try to predict outcomes of what they see and hear. In doing this they are handicapped by their lack of experience, by their unawareness of what is relevant in a particular happening, and by their inability to handle the complexities of multiple causes and different viewpoints. They also have not learned to test their conclusions. Perhaps the greatest incentive to pondering causes and predicting outcomes comes from a young child's encounters with natural phenomena—balls bounce, blocks bang, and bottles break when they fall. Why?

FROM MAGIC
TO NATURAL PHENOMENA

What an infant or young child *thinks* about the nature of the physical world can only be inferred from what he does, what he says, and what question he asks. Because a 6-month-old baby does not look for a ball he has just seen covered, it is assumed that he thinks it no longer exists. At a later age, when he lifts the cover to get the ball, it is assumed that he now knows objects have independent existence. When he counts out two rows of five beads and then says "Five in a row 12 inches long are more than five in a row 6 inches long," it is similarly assumed that he has no idea of the constancy of numbers. When he gives magical explanations of natural phenomena, it is assumed that they are as unaccountable to him as the whimsies of Wonderland were to Alice. Like Alice, young children are not always helped by what they hear.

In a nursery school in which children had been playing with pint and quart measures, a quart of water was poured into a wide, shallow Pyrex dish, with a red line marking the water level. After a warm weekend, the children returned to school to find that the water level had sunk. "Where had the water gone?" "Someone drank it," one child volunteered. "The playroom was locked," the teacher said, "no one could get in." "Batman could," said a young television viewer.

What the children lacked here was the kind of experience that would make the phenomenon of evaporation meaningful to them. So the teacher said, "Let's see what happens when we heat this water on the heating unit. First, though, let's put a blue line at the water level." The water was soon bubbling and a film of steam arose. "What's that?" asked the teacher pointing to the film. "It's too hot to put a finger in, but here's a cold spoon someone could put in the steam." "What's in the spoon now?"

After a pause. "Is the water still up to the blue line?" After another pause. "Where do you think some of the water went?" "Yes, it went into the air. It evaporated."

Enlightening experience is not always so readily at hand. Some years ago I was sitting in the backseat of a car with 3-year-old Eleanor from Nebraska, who was having her first view of the sea as we drove around the San Francisco Bay Area coastline. As we skirted an inlet at low tide, she gave a puzzled look at a stranded boat tied to a pier. "Why," she asked, "is the boat tied?" She had seen a horse tied to a post, but horses run around. A rowboat does not. To answer this question meaningfully would have taken 24 hours, during which Eleanor could have seen the water now far out come slowly lapping in over the mud flat, setting the rowboat bobbing on its surface. She would then have had to see the water slowly recede, uncovering the mud-flat and leaving the boat stranded. Then in again, out again, with all the smells and sights of seabirds skimming the water at high tide, foraging for food in the mud flat at low tide.

To understand natural phenomena, young children need first of all firsthand experiences that are interesting and involving.

Provide experiences with physical forces, simple machines, liquids and gases, sound, heat, light, magnetism, and electricity.

PHYSICAL FORCES In a reasonably well-equipped nursery school, a child sees the block tower he builds on an unsteady base fall to the floor with a bang. He sees the leaves of the trees drift quietly down. The swing he sits on comes gradually to rest even after the biggest push. The tricycle he rides on gathers speed as he pedals downhill. He gives his ball a mighty throw and sees it form an arc through the air as it comes back to the ground. He gets a rough jolt when his wagon runs into the wall and bounces back.

The child's physical experience of the force of gravity, of acceleration and momentum, of action and reaction leads him to take them into consideration. He learns not to let go of his wagon on a hill and not to take blocks up into the tree house or jungle gym because of the possibility of their falling. What he learns to know through sensory experiencing, he will later recognize as intelligible principles (as Galileo and Newton did).

SIMPLE MACHINES A young child can have some experience with all the simple machines: levers, pulleys, inclined planes, gears, and wheels. He can see for himself that when he shifts his hand farther from the head of the hammer, he gets more force in driving a nail or pulling one out with the claws. He can find that to balance his friend on the teeter-totter, he has to adjust his position to the weight on the other side. He learns from his own trucking operations that it is easier to carry blocks in a wagon than to drag them along the ground; that it is easier to push them up a ramp than to carry them up. He can see, too, that the energy he puts into pedaling turns the tricycle wheels.

LIQUIDS AND GASES   A young child loves to pour and mix liquids. He is intrigued by what sinks and floats in water. He is also intrigued by sucking lemonade through a straw, by emptying a fish pond with a syphon, and by blowing bubbles. He also likes to blow up a balloon and take his finger off to see it collapse. When he takes a trip to a nearby service station, he can see flattened tires blow up hard when air is pumped in. In all these experiences, he gets some notion of what happens when pressure is exerted on liquids and gases.

SOUND   Given a chance to drum with his fingers on metal and wooden objects, a child produces different sounds. The song he hears played on the violin has a different quality from the same song played on the piano. A glass full of water has a different sound when tapped than a glass half full or a quarter full. The production, pitch, intensity, and tone quality of sounds become part of a child's experience.

HEAT   A child rubs his hands together on a cold day. He feels them burn when he comes down a rope, gripping it tightly all the way. He moves into the sun to get warm; he burns himself when he touches the hot radiator; he feels the warm air rise from the hot-air register and gradually warm the room; he sees the picnic coffee packed in a thermos to keep it hot; he wraps himself in his blanket to keep warm. He sees milk boil over and a mist of steam rise from the boiling water; he plays with his mother's perfume, leaves the stopper out, and finds it is all gone a few days later. He sees his crayons melt in the sun and the steam change to water on the bathroom window. He shivers in wet clothes and says it feels cold when he has alcohol put on his skin. He sees the milk freeze and rise up like a candle from the bottle. He helps make ice cream and sees salt put in the ice to make the ice cream colder. He sees food kept cold in the refrigerator.

Transference of heat, expansion caused by heat, changes of

state with heat, freezing and cooling caused by evaporation, and heat produced by friction are phenomena that can enter into a child's daily experience.

LIGHT   A child can see a stick bent in the water, pull it out, and find that it is not bent at all. He can hold a small mirror to the sun and play with the reflected beam, shining it on the wall. He can see a spider develop into a fuzzy monster under his magnifying glass. The prisms hanging in the sun glow with jeweled colors. And the kaleidoscope makes ever changing designs as he looks through it in different parts of the room. And so he gets experience with reflection and refraction of light.

MAGNETISM   A magnet and some steel filings give a child a chance to find out what is magnetic and what is not and can lead to ongoing interest in what things are made of.

ELECTRICITY   At home a child sees electricity used as a source of light and power. And when his flashlight stops working, he learns that it needs a new battery.

Random experiences are, though, not enough to help a child when he encounters a new phenomenon. A little boy talking to his grandmother while she was dressing looked at her flabby upper arm. "Gran," he said with memories of service station stops, "you need some air in your arms." At a time when age groups are becoming increasingly segregated, the influence of air on tires may be more a part of a young child's experience than that of age on upper arms. But, unless a child is interested in what he sees or hears, experiences of any kind may make no impression on him. I was reminded of this when driving along an English country lane one summer. My host said, "You see what that is?" I saw a puff of smoke at one side of a field. Something moved across the field. The smoke died down. Then a puff arose at the other side. Something moved with snorts and cranks. I had no idea that what I was looking at were two traction engines, one each side of a field, using steam to draw a plow across by a cable. From early childhood, I had heard of "sounding like a traction engine" used to describe unacceptable noise-making and had probably used the term myself without any understanding of what it meant—until my attention was drawn to two traction engines in appropriate action.

Answer a child's question in terms he understands. Because what a young child is interested in knowing about usually leads to his asking questions, answering questions in terms a child understands is another way of helping him understand natural phenomena. A trusted adult's answer or explanation becomes a part of a young child's understanding. Answer with care.

In a nursery school, some children were playing with a ball that dropped down a crack in a porch undergoing repair and rolled under the house. The children made various futile attempts to reach it, until I told them that tomorrow I would bring my walking stick and that they could push it under the house and hook out the ball. Unfortunately, I forgot my promise. Next morning one of the 4-year-old boys asked me, "When is tomorrow?" Wishing to relate the sequence of events that would mark the passage of time, I said, "When you go home after lunch, you will have your nap. Then you will get up and play. After supper, you will go to bed. Then, when you wake up in the morning, it will be tomorrow."

"And that's the day you bring your walking stick," the little boy said. With a flash of remembrance and contrition, I realized the hopelessness of further explanation, and one tomorrow was lost forever.

Since a young child does not necessarily look at what can be seen, listen to what can be heard, or think about either, and since answers to his questions may be misleading, is there a better way for him to make some sense of natural phenomena?

Devise means for a child to discover cause-and-consequence relationships himself. In a *Creative Playthings* catalog is a picture of a baby pulling a bright-colored wooden knob attached to connecting cords, knobs, a bell, and a chime. His pull makes another knob strike a bell, the bell rings, the chime chimes, and the baby has a gleam of mastery in his eye. He might well be thinking, "To make the bell ring, I pull the knob." Bringing about an interaction of this sort makes children curious and exploratory. It also makes them try to guess what causes what. This is what Dick did (page 15) when trying to figure out why a baby called Kathleen had teeth, whereas another baby not called Kathleen was toothless. This is also what a scientist does before he sets up an experiment. He draws on his experience and knowledge and makes an educated guess. The difference between the scientist's and the young child's guess is that the young child's is intuitive. But, as it is a stage in solving any problem, a child's guessing or conjecturing should be encouraged and his attention drawn to what he may have overlooked or does not know. How important educated guessing is to a scientist is suggested by Sir Peter Medawar, Director of the Royal Institute of Research in England. He recently said that over 80 percent of the time spent in research at the institute could have been saved if the investigators could immediately have thought of the *right* guess or hypothesis to test. The Russian scientist Pavlov similarly emphasized the importance of imaginative guessing as a part of the scientific process. After the Bolshevik Revolution, when fairy tales were banned in Russia as a bourgeois invention, Pavlov pointed out that, without fairy tales, there might be no scientists because a scientist has to imagine what no one else has yet thought of.

Once a child feels free to guess and speculate, he can be encouraged to test his guess. This is what a 3-year-old did (page 188) when he said "I have proof. There *is* a bottom to the sandbox."

Here is an illustration of how a teacher in a San Francisco Children's Center led young children from conjecturing that anything associated with a happening might cause it to having a basis for selecting what is relevant. Note the teacher's use of encouraging interest, questions, provision of material, demonstration, and outlet for application of what was learned.

While children were sitting in a story group, John noticed a mobile, hung from the ceiling above, was spinning. "Look," said John pointing, "it's moving!" "How come?" said another child. "Someone must have touched it," said Mary. "Stand up Mary and see if you can touch it," added the teacher, standing up and reaching herself. "I can't reach it either." "Maybe it spins itself," contributed Bill. "No, it can't spin itself," said another child. "Let's see," said the teacher. She got a piece of yarn with a bead tied to the end and held it out in front of the children. It was still. She then held it near the mobile, which was in the draft of a window. The string swayed gently. "The window, the window is open," suggested the children. "Yes, wind is coming through the window," said John. "And making it move," said all the children, pleased with their discovery. The teacher held the string so the children could blow at it. "Look, I'm the wind," said one of them. That afternoon, outside, the children were given crepe paper streamers to explore wind direction. They were also read *Gilberto and the Wind,* which tells what happens when wind blows the sail of a boat, the arm of a windmill, the smoke from the chimney, and a child's hat and hair.[4]

An experience of this sort gives young children who are born experimenters anyway, a taste for the scientific process which is essentially hypothetico deductive in nature, calling first for a hypothesis or guess based on experience and observation, then a means of testing the guess, and, finally, interpreting the results of the test. What children are likely to guess about or test will naturally be something they are interested in. This

[4]San Francisco Unified School District, "Spinning mobile," *op. cit.,* p. 29.

will vary with the children's experience. Since most children like to play with water and possibly have some experience with dissolving sugar or Jello crystals, mixing powdered paint, or even making cement, 4-year-olds may enjoy an opportunity to find out what sinks, what floats, what dissolves, what is suspended, and what mixes with water or separates from it. All that this requires for a group of four experimenters are four plastic jars with screw tops, a pitcher of water, a cork, a pebble, a package of sugar cubes, a package of poster paint, a bottle of salad oil, an ice cube, a piece of pumice, a box of salt, some sand in a jar, a container of cream, a jar with some orange juice, and some tongue depressors and small spoons. The introduction to experimentation will depend on what the children have recently done with water. They might even be asked what they did with water this morning. This leads easily into, "Let's see some other things you can do with water." Given a choice of what each of them would like to mix with water poured into his or her jar, children have a chance to see that some things float, and some sink and to conjecture why they sink or float. This can lead to weighing them. They can also see that some form solutions and some suspensions; that some liquids mix with water and some separate; and that, when shaken up, those that separate form an emulsion. Giving each child an outline drawing of a jar of water makes it possible for him or her to draw what happened when he put the pebble, ice cube, or whatever it was into water.

When a child begins to explain and predict and to test his explanations and predictions and then interpret his test results, he has taken a long step forward in understanding natural phenomena. He has still to learn, though, that what he thinks depends on his viewpoint.

Help children see that there is more than one viewpoint. A bird's-eye view is not the same as a boy's. Until a child is aware that the position or viewpoint of an observer influences some of his observations, he is unaware of their relative validity. A story sometimes helps him. One is about a feast that describes a cow feasting on some corn put out for it. What it left made a feast for some hens. What the hens left made a feast for some ants.

Children's role-taking in houseplay or storekeeping is another way of their becoming aware of different viewpoints. So are experiences with animals and plants that give children some notion of how organisms use and are used by each other in an ecosystem.

FROM BIRDS AND BERRIES
TO ORGANISMS AND ECOSYSTEMS

When a child begins to compare inanimate objects in terms of their characteristics—color, size, shape—he is ready to think about living organisms as a special class of objects with unique characteristics.

But young children growing up in congested urban areas often have little contact with living organisms, plant or animal. For some city children, human beings, insects, and an occasional bird, tree, or plant may be the sum of their experiences. Their first need, therefore, is for firsthand acquaintance with a variety of animals and plants so that they can get some idea of the differences between organisms and inanimate objects.

Look for signs of plant and animal life in the nursery school yard. There are two possibilities for acquainting young children with animals and plants: Bring the plants and animals to the children or bring the children to the plants and animals. Look around the nursery school yard for signs of plant or animal life. You can be greatly helped by the short course for teachers and parents given by local branches of the Audubon

Society in all large urban centers. Following is a charming account of what a gifted teacher and amateur naturalist, Frances Axtell, and her nursery school children saw and learned in their own nursery school yard:

In the sand under our playground slide, a spot quite free from traffic, a mallow plant sprouted all of its own accord. A casual remark, "That little plant must be thirsty," started one of our most successful and delightful nature experiences.

For weeks the little weed received along with its "drinks" a great deal of care and attention. It was often encircled by prone figures of our nursery school children observing and discussing the things that happened to and on and around "our plant."

It grew to be a healthy, sturdy mallow—a foot tall with several stalks. The lobed leaves unfolded, buds formed, the five silky petals twisted in the bud opened into pink flowers an inch across. After the falling of the petals, the circle of seeds developed, looking like a miniature cheese.

A colony of Argentine ants moved in among the roots. The children watched them foraging for food, saw the tiny white eggs and the larvae or "ant babies." They noticed the care with which the "grown-up ants" tended them.

A speck of a spider came and stayed. He would let himself down from one leaf to another on a thread of web and sometimes climb right back up his "rope."

On hot days after watering, it was visited by bees, flies, and several kinds of butterflies, eager for the moisture.

No one had noticed the egg from which a caterpillar hatched. One morning he was just there. With each molt he changed his size and design. He became large enough so that when he lunched on a mallow leaf the children could see that his jaws moved sidewards instead of up and down like theirs. They liked the way he seemed to flow into himself when he went walking on "his plant" which was also "our plant." He pulled the sides of a leaf toward each other and made a webby covering across the open space beneath which he safely "napped."

With the last molt we put him in a cage with some of his leaves where he could safely pass the time it would take for him to grow up into a butterfly. On the second day he attached himself to the cage ceiling with a bit of web and the "prickly looking" brown and dusty yellow caterpillar became a brown chrysalis with a few gold spots. He was gently sprayed with water every day so he would have sufficient fluid in him to expand his wings properly.

On the sixteenth day the skin of the chrysalis split, the butterfly emerged, wings wet and crumpled. The fanning process, watched by fascinated youngsters, took quite a long time. Finished at last, he was a bright, crisp, sprightly Western Lady, orange with black spots and white and a few pale blue ones near the outer margins of the hind wings—a very common butterfly but our most special one.

For a few drops of watery syrup he unrolled his coil of a tongue, stirred with it and sucked through it as though it were "a drinking straw." The children remembered how he had "chewed leaves when he was a baby." Then, "Goodbye" and away he flew in the sunshine to find his own food and friends and to live his own life the way he was meant to do.

From just-hatched, leaf-chewing caterpillar to nectar-drinking butterfly, the children had witnessed the miracle of metamorphosis. A hard word with real meaning was added to growing vocabularies.

This coming together of different forms of life under natural conditions not only held the children's interest for a long time but was the source of intellectual stimulation and considerable aesthetic enjoyment which they shared with each other. They thought, wondered, and talked about plant life and animal life, the fact of "dead living things" and things that were "never alive." These basic concepts were sorted out and discussed by several philosophical 4-year-olds.

As the days passed, observation became more acute. Noticed were—the iridescent "rainbow wings" of the tiny flies that visited the plant (our 6-inch prism had provided experience with the spectrum); the fact that a drop of water acted as a very small magnifying glass, the leaf veins beneath the drop appearing larger than those around it (a magnifying glass was a familiar tool); even the different colors in the grains of sand from which the flower grew were noted with surprised pleasure.

The ability to express verbally their observation improved markedly in several children, who became more fluent with an enlarged vocabulary.

Perhaps the most valuable part of this experience was the quality of the children's attitude toward the little weed and the insects that found it useful or depended on it. It was one of possessive, protective, interested involvement. The plant became "his plant" (the caterpillar's) as well as "our plant." In a very simple, fundamental way there was a sort of ecological understanding that many forms of life share our earth, that they have different ways of living and somehow depend on each other. The fact that they could so willingly let the butterfly go certainly showed an appreciation of his needs as well as an understanding that butterflies lay eggs that hatch into caterpillars that turn into butterflies, etc. We need to encourage this attitude and these understandings in our children for the sake of their own futures on our beautiful but dwindling planet.[5]

If your nursery school yard offers no signs of plant and animal life and if a bird feeder and bath attracts no feathered visitors, the choice then is what sort of animals to bring in, how long to keep them, how to house them, and how to help children learn something about them.

Provide for short visits by different animal species most likely to be encountered by the children. Over the years I have seen children greatly enjoy visits from a teacher's horse brought in a horse trailer for a day in the nursery school; a mounted policeman's horse; a student's Seeing Eye dog; a goat and a lamb from a farm several miles out in the country; the custodian's talking parrot; crabs from Fisherman's Wharf; worms, slugs, salamanders, and garter snakes from my garden; frogs, lizards, and shellfish picked up on weekend walks; rats and mice loaned from a university biology department. Letting friends and parents know you are interested in "nature experiences" should keep you well supplied with a changing selection of animal visitors.

Prepare appropriate accommodations for animal visitors. If the animals as well as the children are to enjoy these visits, provisions must be made for their comfort and protection from vigorous handling or poking. A standard piece of nursery school equipment could well be an animal house that provides a covered retreat for the animal as well as a ranging area enclosed in a mesh screen. Suitable food must also be provided.

[5]Frances Axtell, "Science is where you find it," *Northern California Association for Education of Young Children Bulletin* (Spring 1966), pp. 17–18.

Prepare children for each animal visit. A young child with no experience with household pets is likely to consider a small animal a toy to be manipulated. In the early days of Head Start programs, many small animal visitors came to an untimely end due to the children's rough and destructive handling. To protect the animals and to give the children some feeling for forms of life different from their own, it is wise to show pictures and filmstrips of prospective animal visitors in their natural habitat. This is a good time to talk over with the children what can be done to make the animal comfortable and gives them some feeling in advance for "looking after" an animal visitor.

Encourage observation and comment rather than immediate handling. If an animal is first seen in an enclosed, screened space with only as many children around as can see well, attention is necessarily focused on what can be seen, heard, and smelled. The way it moves, the sounds it makes, the way it eats, what it eats, and how it looks—big or small, furry or feathered, four legged, whiskered, tailed—are all natural beginning observations best made by each child in his own words. Only when children's comments do not cover all that can be seen is it necessary for a teacher to ask questions.

Ask questions to direct attention to what children overlook. "Does the guinea pig have a tail?" "Is it a tail wagger?" "How many legs has the rabbit?" "Who has more legs—the rabbit or you?" "Can you make a noise like the lamb?" "Can you move like the worm? are questions that may help expand children's observations.

Demonstrate gentle handling. A rabbit's fur can be felt in a gentle stroke. A frog's cold skin can be touched with a finger. A teacher's low, soft voice suggests that more can be seen and heard when an observer is quiet. Squeezing, squashing, and screaming hurt and frighten animals and prevent a child from learning what he might about them.

Introduce recordings of bird, frog, and animal sounds. Because animals are not always vocal under observation, some of the excellent recordings of their sounds can help children get to know more about them.

Show children the uses people make of animals. Children can see, once they are mounted, that a horse is to ride. If the Borden cow makes a morning visit, they can also see that a cow is to milk. They can then help to make butter, ice cream, cottage cheese, and yogurt from cow's milk. When they hatch chicks, they can be shown a film of a poultry farm with eggs being collected, sorted, and sent to market.

As for Seeing Eye dogs, some nursery school children were so impressed by what a blind student told them about her Seeing Eye dog that they offered to be a Seeing Eye dog for her and took her around the nursery school yard by the hand. They treated the dog like a fellow student, talking to him and telling him what was to be seen. After a lamb's visit, they got some wool, borrowed carders, carded the wool, spun it, dyed it, and then wove it on a small kindergarten loom.

Provide experience with animal life cycles. Moths', frogs', and chickens' life cycles lend themselves to brief ongoing observation. Following is an account of some nursery school children's experience with the life cycle of chickens. In addition to what the children learned about the chicken's life cycle, they also had a variety of experiences with the measurement of time, temperature, weight, and length. Note the teacher's provision of materials, her use of questions and visual records, her supplementary use of books and stories, and the children's active involvement throughout the project.

On the first day at nursery school after an Easter vacation during which the 4-year-olds had been exposed to calculated conceptual confusion concerning rabbits, eggs, and chickens, their teacher said, "Instead of a story today we're going to see a movie (*The Red Hen*) of a hen hatching chicks from eggs." When they were comfortably settled, the teacher held up a carton containing three small white eggs and one large one. "Here are some hens eggs," she said. "I got them from the grocery. Are they all the same?" Then replacing the large white with a brown egg the size of the three white ones, she asked, "Are these all the same?" With the children's attention thus alerted to differences in size and color, she said, "Now we're going to see a movie of another kind of hen's eggs." After the film she asked, "Would you like to see some chicks hatch from eggs here in nursery school?" Since they enthusiastically would, "First we'll have to get the *kind* of hens eggs chicks hatch from. Do you know *where* we can get eggs that chicks hatch from?" Grocery eggs, she pointed out, after the children made this suggestion, are only for eating. Since no one knew, she told them hatching eggs came from a hatchery, and together they agreed that an assistant would get six the next day that would be ready to hatch on Thursday. This raised the problem of a way to keep the eggs warm. A hen? No, they couldn't have a hen (residential restrictions). There were, though, on a nearby table a box with a glass top and an electric cord attachment, a light bulb, some wood shavings, and a sponge and bowl of water. "There's a box," said the teacher, feeling with her hand, "but it's not warm. What can we do to make the box warm?" (The teacher ran her hand reflectively along the electric cord.) "The cord," a boy said, "could be plugged in and there was a light bulb." All agreed that, plugged in, the box began to feel warmer, but what to do to make the air moist? This took time to think over. Making a soft nest was a much easier problem, with the shavings so close to hand and eye.

When the children returned to the playroom they saw two posters that duplicated their experience with the size and color of eggs. Both were clearly labeled "four eggs." Had the children asked a question about the difference between grocery and hatchery eggs, the distinction given would have been in terms of one kind being made by a hen, the other kind by a hen and a rooster.

On the second day there was a calendar on the wall with 21 squares, each containing an egg. When the assistant arrived she was asked how many days the eggs had been hatching. Nineteen were scratched off on the calendar. This left two to go, Wednesday and Thursday. "But," said the teacher, as the children counted out the eggs before putting them in the box, "how can we tell if our box will keep the eggs *as warm* as a hen does? What do we *use* to find how warm the day is, the room is, and how warm you are?" The children already had experience with an outdoor thermometer and with clinical thermometers, so this was easy, especially as the teacher marked the *point* the red line would have to rise to for the box to be as warm as a hen. By this time all the children had first-hand experience with the function of an incubator, so the teacher asked, "Do you know what a warm box for hatching eggs is called?"

Since interest was high in what was inside the eggs, a display of color pictures from *Life* magazine was poured over, and at story time *The Golden Egg Book* by Margaret W. Brown was read to knowledgeable listeners.

On the third day, while the children checked the height of the red line in the thermometer and the water in the dish, some of which had gone the same place as water goes from wet clothes drying in the sun, the teacher said, "These chicks won't have a mother to look after them. What can we do for them?" This led to putting a screen over the light bulb and getting out two dishes for mash and water and counting the holes to be sure each chick would have a place to feed and drink. At story time the children enjoyed the joke of Dr. Seuss's Horton (an elephant) hatching an egg. After all, they were doing this, themselves, and better.

On the fourth day interest was at a high pitch. How many chicks out? How many still to hatch? Which do you think will be next? Why? can you see any cracks in the egg? Can you hear a chick peeping inside an egg? One egg remained inert, no crack, no movement, no peeping. Could the chick be dead? The teacher pried off a piece of shell. "Is this chick dead?" she asked. "How do you know?" Yes, a dead chick doesn't move, it doesn't eat, it doesn't breathe, and it doesn't feel anything. The quick and the dead were thus operationally differentiated.

On Friday a caretaking check on water, food, temperature, and the number of chicks led to comments on the chicks' appearance. Could they tell them apart? As the teacher said: "When I look at you I can tell Mary from Bill. What could be done to make the chicks look diffeernt?" Nearby paint and brushes suggested a solution. A stripe of poster paint was gently laid on each chick's back. Now the children had Bluey, Blacky, Greeny, Browny, and one they insisted was Tiger. As they took turns holding each one in their hands there were comments on their size and weight as well as their softness. Could they find how tall they were? The measuring rod used for the children's monthly measuring was too big, but the teacher produced a cardboard inch measure with each inch blocked off in a different color. Before they got to the problem of weighing, the teacher drew out a kitchen scale. "Anyone know what this is?" she asked. "A clock," said one of the girls. "Does it make a sound like a clock? Does a clock have a pan?" asked the teacher. A child reached out and laid his hand on the pan. The pointer moved. "A scale," someone shouted. Two metal weights of 3 and 30 grams were put on the pan one at a time to see which moved the pointer more, which was heavier. And then, which chick to weight and measure?—Tiger, of course. As the children were used to seeing their own heights and weights recorded, the teacher had on hand a piece of poster paper, a chick cutout, a cutout of a scale, and an inch measure. All that was necessary was to draw the position of the pointer and count enough inches to cut off and paste the lot on the poster.

The hatching problem was thus completed and recorded. To those clamoring for more weighing, the teacher said; "We could weigh this chick again next Friday. Do you think it will be *heavier* then? Why?"

The interest generated by this project continued after the chicks were sent to a poultry farm to begin a life of egg laying. At this point the children were shown a film of a poultry farm.

This led to more work with eggs, candling eggs, boiling eggs, making meringues and custards, and measuring volume with a measuring cup, and time with a timer. All the while children were using thermometers, scales, a balance, timer, and volume and inch measures in different brief projects of their own devising, and were recording their outcome by pictographs. Later, frogs' eggs and silkworm eggs were hatched.

In all of this, the teachers were more active and manipulative than they would have been with older children, because it was necessary to orient attention and screen out distracting stimuli. The children's comments to their parents about "our chicks" suggested, though, that they felt it was their project. One of the chicks died over the weekend and was quietly disposed of by a member of the staff. On Monday when this was briefly mentioned, one of the boys gave both teachers a hard look. "What did you guys do with that chick?" he asked. The two guys immediately realized that senior investigators should not make decisions or take action without consulting their junior collaborators.[6]

Arrange field trips to visit plants and animals in their natural habitat. Experiences with animal visitors can be supplemented by field trips to see animals and plants in their natural habitat.

[6]Catherine Landreth, *Early childhood, op. cit.,* pp. 276–278.

What are field trip possibilities? In some cities, local branches of the American Association of University Women have compiled brief descriptions of interesting nearby places that children can be taken to visit. If this help is not available, asking around, reading the local newspaper, and making inquiries about park and recreational facilities may uncover possibilities. Even a nearby pet shop may be worth consideration. In all field trips, a preliminary visit by the teacher is necessary to assess what will be of interest and to plan ways of preparing the children for what they will see. In Berkeley, a nursery school trip to the yacht harbor and marina was led up to by bringing in driftwood, seaweed, seawater, starfish, and a variety of shells. A film was shown of the sea, and during rest time Debussy's *La Mer* was played for the children. With this preparation and thoughtful transportation planning, children had some idea in advance of what they might see and look at. On the trip they bought some clams at the fish market and returned to nursery school to steam and eat them. A few days later, there were photographs on the bulletin board to remind them of what they had seen. Together with the teacher, they made up a story of their adventure.

Follow-up and recall are as helpful in a field trip as preparation. So are such related experiences as pictures, stories, films, sound recordings, and classification games.

Devise simple species-classification games. Sorting or matching games of a lotto type that require putting all the birds, the fish, the insects, and the worms into piles is one suggestion. Another is finding, in a set of pictures, the appropriate mother or home for pictured young animals.

Provide a variety of experiences with plants. Plants, though not as interesting to young children as animals, can also be brought within children's experience and interest through the use they make of them. Helping to prepare lunch can include podding peas and scrubbing carrots. Decorating the Christmas tree can lead to popping corn and stringing cranberries. Children can also grow carrots, tomatoes, and other vegetables (in containers if no garden plot is possible). The watering and care of whatever they grow give them some idea of growth needs. Planting bulbs and cuttings as well as seeds also gives them the idea that not all plants grow from seeds.

Make decorative use of plants. Children can learn, too, to enjoy plants as decoration if a teacher or parent can spare some time for container gardening, using a variety of succulents, bulbs, and flowering plants. The beauty of teasels, goldenrod, thistles, dock, and autumn leaves can be preserved by putting their stalks in glycerin before arranging them in boxes or baskets. There are many ways in which the beauty of plant forms can be made a part of a young child's environment, regardless of inner-city limitations.

Seek accurate information and use correct terms. In presenting experiences to young children, a teacher needs first to have a naturalist's eye for living things. She also needs accurate information so that she does not misinform children when they ask questions. In making simple explanations, the use of exact terminology paves the way for a child's later learning. So call a gill a *gill,* a pupa a *pupa,* and a kid a *kid.* Seek, too, information from reliable sources, from encyclopedias, from botany and zoology textbooks, and from such science curriculum improvement studies as the one at the University of California. Though science curricula usually begin at kindergarten age, they are helpful because they represent years of thoughtful planning and testing by scientists, teachers, and developmental psychologists and because some of the projects lend themselves to simple adaptations for prekindergarten naturalists.

FROM LINES, DAUBS,
AND SMEARS TO PICTURES

In the Gesell Infant Developmental Schedule, test items for 12-month-old infants are "to hold a crayon adaptively, to make a stroke, and to imitate a stroke; At 18 months of age, a test item is "to scribble spontaneously and vigorously."[7] By the time a 2-year-old child enters a children's center, he enjoys and is eager to make marks on paper. A 3-year-old I know responds to any parental thwarting with a dark look and, "I won't make you a picture tomorrow." Are there recognizable stages in a child's progress from scribbles to pictures?

Rhoda Kellog, who has collected over a million drawings and paintings of young children in different parts of the world, believes there are. In a charming book, *The Psychology of Children's Art* (C.R.M. Random House, 1967), she presents a selection of drawings and paintings that supports her belief that young children all over the world draw the same. She analyzes in their drawings 20 "basic scribbles" that include vertical, horizontal, diagonal, circular, curved, and waving lines in repetitive patterns. She also finds an almost equal number of ways in which children place their scribbles on a piece of paper—using only one-quarter of a page, centering their scribbles, placing them on a diagonal axis, or in a variety of other arrangements. These basic scribbles and placement patterns are the elements of all young children's pictures.

Around 3 years of age, most children develop the ability to enclose space with a line. Copying a circle is a test item in the Stanford-Binet for 3-year-olds.[8] When a child can make circles, ovals, squares, rectangles, triangles, crosses, and free-form space enclosures, his pictures increase in variety and complexity. As he combines these space enclosures, they some-

[7]Not all children can or necessarily should be able to do this at these ages.
[8]See footnote 7.

times suggest something he knows—a car, a house, a man, or an animal. From this stage, it is but a step to planned pictorial representation.

Two 4-year-olds, John and David, were standing by an easel. It was the week before Christmas. John said to David, "I'll make you a picture." As he painted, he said, "This is the baby Jesus." David asked, "Is he a real person?" "Yes," said John, sketching in a round body, "he has a stomach." "Now," John said, "I'll draw the Virgin Mary," and he began a head in blue. "Is she a real person?" asked David, "does she have a stomach?" "Yes," replied John, "Jesus was in her stomach." John completed the second figure, picked up another brush and said, "Now, I'll draw God." "Is he a real person?" asked David. "No," said John, drawing this time only a head and then removing his painting to the wire to dry.

A young child's painting and drawing is necessarily a self-taught art. Its development reflects a child's progressive eye–hand coordination of movement. Process and product are inseparable because most of the time a young child does not know what he is painting until he has laid down his brush. What his creation will be depends on how it may turn out. What can you do to help a child in such an endeavor? In brief, you can provide the materials he needs, help him become independent in their use, and leave him be. But, more can be said about materials.

Provide materials for crayoning, chalking, brush and finger painting. A young child's pleasure and progress in drawing and painting depend largely on having the materials he needs conveniently at hand.

CRAYONING REQUIRES:

Sturdy sheets of paper, manila or newsprint, 8-by-12 inches or 12-by-18 inches, which can be spread out on a table or floor or pinned to a wall or easel.

A basket of jumbo crayons about three-quarters of an inch in diameter suited to the coordination of small fingers.

CHALKING CALLS FOR:

Paper or a blackboard and eraser.
A container full of colored chalks.
If a child likes the result he gets with wet paper, stacks of wet paper can be put out on a tray.

BRUSH PAINTING makes somewhat more preparation demands on a teacher until the children learn to prepare the paints themselves. It calls for:

Two easels with two blunt-tipped nails protruding near each upper corner.
Sheets of paper (18-by-24 inch newsprint) with two holes punched to correspond with the position of the nails for easy slipping on and off.
Three or four jars of poster paint, clean and fresh each morning.
A well-washed brush in each jar.
A nearby drying line.

FINGER PAINTING CALLS FOR:

Butcher paper.
Some convenient means of damping it.
Two or three jars of finger-paint paste colored with vegetable dye. Basically, paste is a combination of 1 part of flour to about 2 1/2 parts of water, beaten and cooked until it is clear and then cooled.
A tier of meshed wire racks, like those used in drying fruit, takes care of drying the painting.
Some kind of smock or apron for each painter.
A nearby sink and running water for washing hands and wiping off the table surface.

Since the preparation for and putting away after painting requires water, it is only logical to group art activities in a part of the playroom that has running water, a child-height bench for preparation, and low storage shelves for the materials in daily use.

Help children learn how to use art media. At the painting easel, it may help a novice to see that if he wipes his brush on the side of the jar, the paint will not drip or run; that keeping each brush in its own paint jar keeps the color clear; and that color can be mixed on paper by brushing one color over another. A child who continues to use only his palms and wrists in finger painting may not be averse to a suggestion that he could use his fingers too, if he wishes. Show each child where to hang his painting and where to get a cloth to wipe up. Remind him to wash his hands before pulling off his smock, if this is necessary.

Limit comments on children's pictures to obvious characteristics of color and shape. Asking a child if his picture is a house, a dog, or whatever is pointless when he may simply be experimenting with lines and boundaries. If you must say something to show your interest, a few words about the color of the painting, the stripes, or the circles avoids misinterpretation. Asking a child to tell you about his painting may confuse him also if he thinks the painting speaks for itself.

Help make children independent in preparing art materials and clearing away. Have running water, a workbench, and paint supply shelves at child height. In some centers, you may need to provide a stool or steps to bring the children up to an adult-height sink.

Paint a permanent colored ring around each paint jar to mark the amount of mixed paint to be made for each day.

Provide a *scoop* that measures the right amount of paint

powder and a *measuring cup* that holds just the amount of water needed to reach the mark on the paint jar.

Pin, at a child's eye level, a pictograph instruction sheet that shows, in left-to-right order:

A scoop of powder.
A measure of water.
The two combined into a paste with the use of a tongue depressor.
Water added up to the mark on the paint jar.

Make labels for each jar of poster paint with a strip of red paper clearly printed *red* and the same for each other color.

Have brushes always well washed and in good condition, so the need for their care and washing is more obvious to the children.

Demonstrate both the preparation of paints and the kind of wiping up and washing needed in clearing away, using simple statements to direct attention to what is being done.

Sign and preserve a sample of each child's painting in his own folio with his name on it. Signing a child's painting with his initials suggests that it is a product. Preserving and enhancing his product by flattening his finger paintings and using hair spray on some of his wet chalk-paintings is similar recognition; so is suggesting he take some of his paintings home and occasionally displaying an attractive painting suitably matted and hung at a child's eye level in the nursery school. A representative folio of each child's paintings and drawings records his progress in the use of color and design, mastery of line, and attempts at pictorial representation.

Provide parquetry sets to give supplementary experience with color combinations. Since no techniques are involved in the use of this medium, a child's attention can be concentrated on color, composition, and design.

Introduce collage materials to give children experience with texture. Children who have had considerable experience with crayons and chalks, brush and finger paints, and who have the coordination for pasting may enjoy giving texture to their designs and compositions. All that is needed are sheets of plain or colored manila or construction paper, paste jars and brushes, and a varied collection of collage materials. Begin with just a few of these, such as paper shapes of different colors and small scraps of cloth, so that children can experiment with form and color combinations before being distracted by a wide range of feathers, tinsel, tinfoil, string, yarn, and whatever. In time, each child may wish to develop his own collage collection.

Provide blocks and clay for three-dimensional experience with form and design. Harriet Johnson's *The Art of Block Building* presents a number of sketches of the types of constructions and arrangements some young children made with a set of blocks designed by Caroline Pratt. These blocks (in a variety of shapes besides rectangular units, cubes, and cylinders) vary in dimension in such a way that each is a fraction or multiple of some other block of the same shape. The variety in shape and the dimension relationships suggest possibilities for all sorts of spatial arrangements. All that is needed for their free use is:

Adequate shelf storage and a floor area that provides enough working space and freedom from interference from other activities.

A carpet square for building on defines the building area and makes block work quieter.

A pasted or painted outline of each kind of block on the back of the shelf where each belongs promotes orderly putting away and draws children's attention to the differences in shape and dimension of the blocks.

Photographs of interesting block designs made by the children can be put on the bulletin board so that each child has some record of a construction he enjoyed making.

Though a young child's muscle coordination limits what he can do with clay, its malleability makes it possible for him to change one form into another: a sphere into a cylinder, a flattened disk into a bowl. A simple way of preparing clay is to suspend clay powder in a flour sack in a basin or bowl of water for 24 hours or until the clay is completely damp. Once this is worked into small balls for children's use, it must be kept covered if it is not to dry out. Covered crocks or plastic bags make satisfactory containers. The table surface it is worked on should, obviously, be one that is easy to clean.

Children get a better idea of the possibilities of this medium if some of their products are fired and if they can take a field trip or see pictures of the kiln in which it is fired, as well as some of the stages in making a simple bowl—before firing, after firing, before glazing, and after the glaze is baked on. Photographing some of the children's clay models and then putting up the photographs on the bulletin board gives them a record of what has been done and can be done with clay.

Plan for visual delight as well as practical usefulness in children's surroundings. A young child's growing awareness of color, design, composition, and texture should lead to his increasing enjoyment of his environment. Art activities are as much training in seeing as in creating. But, is his environment planned with this in mind?

Select furnishings, equipment, and all that the child sees in the nursery school with an eye to what it offers in color, design, composition, and texture. A teacher is also an aesthetic part of the setting. What she wears and how she looks does not escape the children's attention. A Standard-Binet test item at 4.6 years is to show the children two sketches of a woman's head and ask them which is the prettier.

In the twenties, I conformed to a nursery school convention of wearing a cotton smock and "sensible" shoes in a college nursery school. I did not care for the way I looked in this outfit. Apparently, the children felt the same way. One morning when I was going out to a lunch meeting, I appeared during the children's rest period in a dress and street shoes. As I left, I overheard one of the girls say, "Miss L. has on her good dress today." A boy said, "Yes, she has on her good shoes, too." The little girl replied with a sigh, "My Sunday school teachers wear more prettier dresses than my college teachers,"—a telling remark that I took to heart with good effect.

FROM MAKING THINGS
TO USING SIMPLE TOOLS
AND DEVELOPING HANDICRAFT SKILLS

A young child likes to make things, from mud pies to make-believes of various sorts—trains and planes, bridges and boats. He is also attracted to tools and machines because he sees adults using them. It is worth recalling that, during the Industrial Revolution, England's economic prosperity depended in part on the machine-tending of young children of the poor. Daniel Defoe, speaking of the children of Yorkshire clothiers, said, "Scarce anything above 4-years old, but its hands were sufficient for its own support."

Although the work of some young children's hands was callously exploited in the nineteenth century, in the late twentieth century young children in favored living circumstances may often feel frustrated in their desire to work with their hands. A billion-dollar play material industry is so busy making things for them that it is a rare child who has much chance to make something for himself. Notice, though, with what pleasure a 3-year-old attaches a piece of string to a kite-shaped piece of paper and casts it hopefully into the breeze, or staples a fringed piece of paper to make an Indian head-dress. Some television programs for young children among them "Misteroger's Neighborhood" and the Australian "Play School," recognize the pleasure that making things gives young children.

In a recent "Play School" half hour, an attractive young Australian who had advised his child viewers what to have on hand for the day, rummaged in a treasure chest, picked out a white Styrofoam-ball, and poked a stick in it. Then, chatting companionably, he made two circles and dots for eyes, a straight line for a nose, curved lines for mouth and chin, and squiggles for hair and eyebrows. All this was done with leisurely deliberation so as not to get ahead of any working viewers. Next, he poked the stick through a hole in a paper-bag dress, counted the four buttons he drew on its front, and held up a puppet. Not Ernie or Bert! ("Sesame Street"). But what satisfaction its making must have given the 3- and 4-year-old Australians who made one for themselves. You do not, of course, have to put on a television program to aid and abet young children in making things. All you need do is provide the makings and the tools and some supervision of their use.

Provide a variety of materials for children's use. Here are just a few:

A bin of soft lumber ends (leftover scraps of lumber) and a
   supply of nails suggest exciting carpentry projects.
Spools can become chimneys or smokestacks.
Wooden buttons can become wheels.
A shoe box with a string attached may be a satisfactory wagon
   for a toddler.

A piece of leather stretched over an open-ended coffee tin
may become a drum.

Feathers stuck in a strip of leather may make a headband.

Paper plates may finish up as masks.

A tangle of yarn can become hair.

Odd felt pieces can become hats.

Beads may become necklaces.

Oddments of string, decorative paper, and strips of carpet
may become who knows what.

Crayons, felt pens, paint, and design stamps may suggest
decorative embellishment.

Most of these materials call for the use of simple tools.

Provide simple tools for children's supervised use. Saws and
hammers and a hard workbench surface to hammer on, a vice
to hold the wood, and a hand drill to make holes require only
a little demonstration and interest and approval for effective
workmanship. Blunt kindergarten scissors, staplers, and
punches for making things with construction paper also call
for a demonstration of their appropriate use at a worktable.
Measuring devices, such as rulers, tape measures, or yard-
sticks should be on hand.

As making things progresses, you will get cues from the
children for a greater variety of materials and simple tools. As
they work with wood in such forms as lumber ends, blocks,
dowels, spools, curtain rings, toothpicks, and sawdust, they
become more aware of the craft possibilities of different
materials. As they hammer, they become selective in their use
of nails, considering their head size and their length. They
learn which holds best—nail, thumbtack, scotch tape, glue, or
paste. So, when they see a carpenter at work, they observe
and question him as a fellow worker of more advanced skill.

*Help children make something (of their own devising) for
daily use.* When children have a chance to make something

that can be put into effective use: a bird-feeding station out of oddments of metal chain, wire, and wood or a wind vane that twirls in the breeze—they become producers as well as consumers. They have a part in making their world.

This is not all they gain. In the evolution of man, the development of the hand and the use of tools had a part in the development of the mind. In our current zeal for accelerated cognitive development, let us not overlook this developmental relationship between hand and mind. Neither let us overlook what satisfying experience in making things may do in generating an interest in crafts to fill some of the leisure that technology promises the rising generation.

FROM BOUNCING TO DANCING

A bouncing baby is a term used to describe a baby in the pink of health. A healthy baby bounces. He bounces to inner rhythms of his own, and he bounces to music with a marked rhythm, though not always in bounce with the rhythm. He also kicks rhythmically and repetitively. When he gets around on foot, his rhythmic activity expands. He drums and strums on resonant surfaces with hands, fingers, and feet. He swings. He pounds. He bounces on the bouncing board and seems to enjoy the rhythm as well as the vigor of his activity. What can be done to increase his enjoyment by making him more sensitive and responsive to rhythmic patterns of sound and movement?

Develop a child's repertoire of rhythmic expressive movements. "Could you show me how the rabbit moves?" "How does the duck move?" asked when a rabbit or a duck are in view, or "how do the gulls fly?" when they are swooping overhead are questions that usually evoke some expressive movement. So are "show me how you hang out the clothes, how you hammer a nail, how you run fast, how you walk very slowly, how you bounce like a ball, how you rock a baby doll, how you reach up to the sky, and how you bend down to touch the ground."

Developing a repertoire of expressive rhythmic movements need not be restricted to a rhythm or music period. It can go on during children's free play outdoors or whenever an opportunity presents itself.

Try dancing without music first. One Sunday I was visited by a college dance instructor, Eleanor, and her 3-year-old son. After lunch and a nap, the son said, "Let's dance, Eleanor." They removed their shoes. I pushed the coffee table out of the way. Thereupon the little boy did a few warming-up stretching exercises he had seen his mother's students do in her studio. Then she asked, "What dance will we do?" He said, "A running dance," and they tripped around lightly poised in graceful rhythmic motion. Next he elected a jumping dance and danced lightly and rhythmically on his toes. In all, he completed six dances before putting on his shoes. All were of his own devising, all were based on movements that were a normal part of a little boy's repertoire. All were charming, reflecting as they did his spontaneity and self-imposed control in rhythmic movement.

Giving a young child a chance to first experience rhythm in his own body movement prepares him for the more complex process of synchronizing his movement with the rhythm of someone else's sound pattern. Incidentally, in modern dance composition, choreography often precedes the selection of a musical accompaniment.

Remove shoes—children's and your own—before dancing. Asking children to remove their shoes before they begin to dance suggests that dancing calls for free feet that can stretch and flex. It also eliminates distracting noise and can strengthen the children's feet muscles.

Introduce simple sound accompaniments to dancing. Once a child has begun a dance, you can accent the rhythm of her running or jumping by clapping your hands and asking the other children, "Who would like to dance? Who would like to clap?" Hand-clapping can lead to exploring other kinds of sounds that children can make with their hands, such as slapping their thighs. Later, bring out a basket of simple percussion instruments: rattles, Mexican maracas, drums, pairs of hollow blocks, and tap sticks. A rhythmic sound accompaniment gives both dancers and accompanists experience with rhythmic repetition, beat, and tempo.

Make a game of recognizing and reproducing rhythmic sound patterns. A record, "Little Indian Drum," which taps out the "talking" an Indian Chief does with the little drum he gives his son, is full of suggestions for ways of encouraging young children to listen to and distinguish between different rhythmic sound patterns.

Tap children's names or "All aboard" or "Come to the cookhouse door, boys" on a drum and ask, after a few demonstrations, if the children know what the drum is saying. Then hand the drum to a child so that he can make it say something for everyone to guess.

Ask children to *listen* to a musical sound pattern and clap it with their hands before getting up to dance. This promotes listening for different rhythmic sound patterns.

Provide simple props to enhance rhythmic movement. A child who may be a little self-conscious about his or her own body movement may be freed by having a scarf to dance with. To make the scarf "dance," a child has to dance too. Ankle or wrist bells are other inducements to dancing.

Accept and encourage children's suggestions and inventions. If dance is to offer a child another medium of expression, he must be free to learn to dance his own way. A charming film with the title *Dance Your Own Way* shows how a dance teacher helped young dancers discover and develop themselves as well as their dance.

What children try to express or what they suggest expressing in dance sometimes reveals odd gaps in their learning. In one dance group made up of 4-year-olds was a child recently emigrated from Austria. She made remarkable progress in picking up the English language. Once, though, when children were improvising running-horse, running-children, and running-rabbit dances, she surprised us by saying, "Now, let's do running noses." What would you have done with that suggestion?

FROM LALLING TO SINGING

By the second half of the first year of life, most babies spend considerable time lalling and crooning, making repetitive sounds of a da-da, mum-mum, ba-ba, ma-ma sort and all with a rhythmic singsong quality. They also experiment with inflection and with differences in pitch.

Two- and three-year-olds also experiment with a variety of sounds: the low-pitched woof of a dog, the throaty roar of a lion, the whine of a plane overhead, and the chug of a train. They often accompany their activity with chanting, repeating over and over, "I'm making a house. You can't come here. Girls keep out." Sometimes, too, they devise a singsong pattern of sound that may or may not have words but may suggest some attempt at a musical phrase and its repetition. They not only enjoy their own singing, they like to be sung to. If they did not, there would not have been such a wealth of nursery songs and lullabys sung to young children over the centuries. So, how do you make song and singing part of the life of a young child?

Two contrasting memories of mine suggest how a child's feeling for song and singing may be influenced by his experience. During World War I, I spent a short time as a teen-aged teaching assistant in a New Zealand primary school. Part of my assisting involved accompanying, on the piano, the weekly singing lesson for a group of 7-year-old children. Their teacher was not much for singing, but it was in the syllabus, so she braced herself for the half hour of song by laying a wooden pointer and a leather strap on the piano. On the blackboard were the words of the song that was to be given at the annual breakup. The song was "Men of Harleck." I have no recollection of why it was chosen nor of any explanation of who the men of Harleck were or why they were rushing to battle. It was enough that "Men of Harleck" was the song the children were to learn to sing to their mothers at the breakup. At our first meeting, the teacher rapped the piano for close attention, pointed to the words on the board, and asked me to play it through once. From there on, like the men of Harleck, we joined in battle. In fact we rarely got far from "march to battle" without a peremptory tapping on the piano and a brief halt while some inattentive or playful child was brought out and strapped. Then another tap of the pointer on the piano, and in somewhat chastened mood, we were all off again.

The breakup finally came. Screened from view by an aspidistra borrowed to give some grace to the occasion, I accompanied the embattled 7-year-olds through two verses of "Men of Harleck": not a word or note out of place. A patter of polite parental applause ended our joint ordeal. What the children's associations were or are with "Men of Harleck" I do not know. To this day I do not care to hear it, reminding me as it does of my unwilling complicity in one of the most discouraging approaches to singing I have heard.

Thirty years later, again in New Zealand, I was seeing off

a young niece on the overnight interisland ferry. Dusk and a light drizzle kept farewelling friends under the dimly lit roof of the wharf shed. The mournful sound of the first whistle lingered in the air as we waited silent and damp, looking up at those we had said good-bye to, too far from us to speak to. At that moment there was a rush of young people on the wharf and a young girl and her mother ran up the gangplank before it was lowered. Their companions, young Hungarians, laughing and talking, surged to the edge of the wharf and, as the girl came on deck, they sang to her in harmony, looking up in her face. When they paused, she sang back to them. What they sang—in German—I do not know. All I know is that the mood of the moment changed. The dusk, the drizzle, and the parting became a setting for song. The singers were refugees far from the country of their origin, but as they sang they seemed to recapture something enjoyed and familiar, something that made us all one.

What can you do to make singing something "every child may joy to hear"?

Encourage and join in with their song improvisation. You may not sing as well as Julie Andrews. Still, there are many moments in a morning when a song can lift spirits and feet: Sing something you have improvised on the spur of the moment to accompany some train, boat, or pounding activity or a snatch of "Polly Perkins, hold on to my jerkin" when one or two children are following each other indoors. Try "Heigh-ho, heigh-ho, It's off to work we go" during the yard cleanup period, or some variant of "Rock, rock, rock, the boat" when children are on the rocking boat. If you do not care for the sound of your voice, some singing lessons might be worth considering.

Being able to carry a tune opens up a new world in listening pleasure and shared group-singing for young children. They particularly enjoy learning to sing a song that their brothers, or parents can sing.

Introduce folk songs and other simple songs of a descending-scale type within children's pitch range. Any song that "folks" sang is for obvious reasons not demanding in pitch range. Following are some songbooks that offer helpful suggestions:

American Folk Songs For Children, by Ruth C. Seegar (New York: Doubleday, 1968).
Animal Folk Songs For Children, by Ruth C. Seegar (New York: Doubleday, 1950).
Singing Time, by Satis N. Coleman and Alice G. Thorn (New York: Day, 1950).
The Little Singing Time, by Satis Coleman and Alice G. Thorn (New York: Day, 1940).

Help children learn to get control of pitch and tone. Do not discourage a young singer because he is not on pitch or in tune. There are, though, some ways of helping him distinguish and reproduce sounds of different pitch. One way is to encourage the use of a soft or small voice. Another is to improvise call-and-answer songs. Try, "What are you doing John? What have you there?" on one note and sing back on the same note with John, "I'm making a boat." Or in a little song group, try, "Good morning little yellow bird . . . who are you?" to which the child replies, "My name is. . . ." Singing a child's name up or down a scale also gives experience in reproducing tones of different pitch.

Introduce a song without instrument accompaniment. For young singers, it is easier to reproduce a song that is not complicated by instrumental accompaniment. It is also easier for children to begin by singing just a line or two, like a chorus. For example, "Nick-nack paddy wack, give the dog a bone," is a good line to begin with in the song, "This old man."

Introduce group singing. Encourage but do not coerce children to come together in a small group to sing. As to how many, four may be a good beginning number for a first attempt. The length of the session depends on the children's interest and enjoyment. Taping the children's singing for playback may give each of them some feeling of their part in a performance.

Choose some songs for language development. Since singing involves words, it can, as has already been suggested, become an adjunct to language development. It would, though, be unfortunate if this were made the exclusive basis for choice of song. After all, most opera patrons do not recognize one word of what they hear sung, unless they know the libretto by heart. The following are some simple songs young children seem to like that serve the development of language.

FOR FOLLOWING VERBAL DIRECTIONS: "Row, Row Your Boat," and such improvisations to this tune as "Clap, Clap, Clap Your Hands," and "Stamp, Stamp Your Feet."

PLURALS: "Oats, Peas, Beans, and Barley Grow."

PAST AND PRESENT TENSE: Change the tenses in "Mary Had a Little Lamb," "Hickory Dickory Dock," and "London Bridge Is Falling Down."

ALPHABET SONG to tune of "Twinkle, Twinkle, Little Star."

COUNTING: "Ten Little Indians," kittens, and so on.

DIRECTION AND RIGHT, LEFT: "Here We Go Looby Loo," "Hokey, Pokey," and "Eency Weency Spider."

RHYMING: "Twinkle, Twinkle Little Star."

Some of these songs are accompanied by action. This combination heightens the emotional release music offers to children.

Make up action songs out of children's interests and activities. "Open them shut them, open them shut them, give a little clap," followed by a variety of hand activity is one way of converting the tedium of a waiting period before lunch into a period of expressive activity and language development. It, incidentally, gets children's hands out of each other's hair. A folk–action song that can be joined in by singers of different ages has the social value of making it possible for young children to enter into a group with a wide age range. A Peace Corps student in Nepal found one of her most successful contributions was teaching young Nepalese "Hokey, Pokey." In no time the children's parents shyly asked her if she would teach them "Hokey, Pokey" too. Ping-Pong is not the only means of bringing national, let alone age, groups together.

FROM HEARING MUSIC
TO LISTENING TO IT

Unless a child listens, music may be little more than background noise. It is only by listening that he becomes aware of tempo, tonality, musical phrases, and the tone quality of different instruments.

Introduce listening music during brief rest periods. Playing music while children are resting before lunch promotes listening because there are no other pressing demands on their attention. What they listen for will depend on their experience with music.

Give children opportunities to see, hear, and touch a few instruments. Children are helped to distinguish between the tone quality of different instruments by occasional visits from a violinist, a cellist, a flutist, or the player of whatever instrument who is willing to spend 10 or 15 minutes showing a small group of children his instrument and how he plays it—by drawing a bow over the strings, by blowing into a tube, or striking the keys of a keyboard. When this is followed by playing some melody that the children know well and then playing a melody particularly suited to the instrument, a child gets some experience with differences in tone quality as well as some notion of how tones of different pitch are produced. This is helped, of course, when the children sing along with an instrumental accompaniment.

Once children have some familiarity with a few different instruments, a recording like "Little Brass Band" or even sections of Prokofiev's "Peter and the Wolf" give interest and pleasure in demonstrating how each instrument's tone quality contributes to any musical ensemble: quartet, symphony, or band.

Expose children to a variety of listening music. Play a variety of music you enjoy yourself: vocal as well as instrumental, quartet and symphony as well as solo, Mozart as well as folk music, Gilbert and Sullivan as well as spirituals. Getting to know a piece of music calls for hearing it many times. So play the same piece on several consecutive days and play it through again if the children seem to enjoy it.

Develop a filed, indexed record collection for convenient selection. Recorded music is more likely to be introduced appropriately if you can quickly lay your hand on a particular record. It is also more likely to be enjoyed if attention is paid to changing the phonograph needle when this is necessary and to discarding records that have lost their original reproduction quality. If the purpose of introducing records is to give children opportunities to hear good recordings of a variety of music, the handling of the records and the record player is best left to the teacher. You can still give children some sense of participation by asking them what they would like.

Refer to recorded music by name. The only way a child can ask for a piece of music he likes, unless he can hum a bar or two, is to remember its name. So, tell the children the name of whatever piece you are playing, ask them if they know the name of a particular piece, and try to remember the favorites of different children.

Devise music listening games. To encourage children to listen to rather than hear music, some variant of musical chairs— marching or running around and stopping when the music stops—at least calls their attention to when the music starts and stops.

Soft, gentle clapping of a rhythm in a pianissimo passage and vigorous clapping of fortissimo make them aware of loud and soft passages.

As for differences in pitch, a record titled "Music Listening Game" offers many suggestions. It invites children to guess whether different familiar sounds: the whistle of a train, the moo of a cow, and the meow of a cat, go *up* or come *down* or *stay the same.*

An introduction to musical phrase might be listening to the clocks in the "Toy Store" or in "Peter and the Wolf," listening to the lilting phrase that represents Peter or the ones that introduce the duck, the cat, the bird, and the wolf.

Encourage appropriate use of some simple musical instruments. What any children's center can offer in the way of musical instruments for use by children will depend not only on its equipment budget but on teachers' knowledge of the availability of instruments suitable for use by young children. These can be classed under (1) instruments of tuned-bar type, (2) drums, (3) gongs, (4) bells, and (5) stringed instruments such as the guitar or autoharp. If a child is to have any musical experience with these, he needs to learn how to use them appropriately as musical instruments, not as manipulative toys. Some idea of the results from this kind of experience is offered in a report and recordings of the music made by children in a school established by the Pillsbury Foundation at Santa Barbara in 1942.

FROM AWARENESS OF OTHERS
TO GETTING ALONG WITH THEM

A glance at the morning papers is enough to convince anyone that we still have a lot to learn about getting along with others. So has a young child. He is, though, early aware of others. Around 6 weeks of age, he smiles at a human face. As he also smiles at a mask of a human face, it is hard to tell what he makes of the faces that bend over him, the voices that speak to him, and the hands that soothe and make him comfortable. He begins, though, to sort them out. By 6 months of age, he saves his smiles for friendly, familiar faces and shows a preference for a particular person. He becomes more selective and sensitive in his response to his human associates. How he responds to them during his first year depends, of course, on how they act toward him, on whether they give him some basis for trusting them and feeling secure in their care and affection.

In getting along with adults, a child under 2 years of age can usually count on their making concessions to his immaturity and need for watchful care. When he goes to a children's center, the children he meets there do not make these concessions. He, therefore, has to learn to meet them on their terms, which are different from those of a caretaking adult.

How can a teacher help a child learn through his own experience that some kinds of social interaction lead to pleasant ongoing activity for all and that other kinds produce disruption and distress? How can she help him sense in others feelings and needs similar to his own? How can she help him learn to balance the demands of companionship against its pleasures, to be part of a group, and yet be his own man?

Ask about a child's experience with adults and children. In chatting with a child's mother during the pre-entry home visit, it is natural to ask whether he has played with other children and whether he likes being with them. He may not. Older children may have teased, bossed, or indulged him; younger ones may have been bossed by him. Playing with children his own age, in the presence of an overprotective mother, may have led to running to mother whenever any difficulty arose.

What a mother says about and to her child gives some clue to his household role: a contributing member, an interruption in his parents' social and professional lives, the household kingpin or whatever. What a mother says also gives some clue to whether her child is talked to, with, or at and in what tone of voice. And a question about his dressing, toilet, and eating habits reveals whether he is expected to do what he can for himself or to anticipate service.

Since "getting along" with others in our society is given a variety of interpretations of what getting along means with *what* others, a casual question, "How does Bill seem to get along with children and adults?" may throw some light on home attitudes toward getting along with what others.

Make a child's first group experiences pleasant. No one, child or adult, is likely to put forth much effort in trying to understand and conform to the wishes and interests of a group of people whom he does not enjoy being with. The child's first need, then, is to enjoy his experiences with others. One way of making them enjoyable is to hold an open house the Saturday or Sunday before new children enter a group. A half-hour visit for each child and his parents in groups of four or five at a time gives both the children and the parents a chance to get better acquanted with the teacher and familiar with the physical facilities of the center and what the child can do there.

Limit the materials available on the first day. Putting out everything on the children's first day in the center may overwhelm or distract them. Some books in the bookrack, two easels set up for painting side by side, a puzzle table, a table for crayoning and one with some soft dough for modeling, an attractive houseplay corner, a block building area, and some new sand toys in the sandbox are enough to bring children together in easy, pleasant groups. There will be time enough later to bring out other resources.

Schedule a short stay with mother present on first morning. Bringing new children into the group about four at a time gives a teacher an opportunity to give each child individual attention and to get some idea of how ready each is to have his mother leave. His mother, meanwhile, has an opportunity to see what goes on in the center. When she leaves, she can help her child by telling him where she is going and when she will be back and by suggesting something he can do, such as "You could make a picture for daddy."

While a teacher is sizing up her new children, they, too, are sizing up their new environment. A 3-year-old boy transfererd from a very permissive play cooperative greeted his mother when she returned for him on his first morning with, "They don't hit here!"

On suceeding days, getting along can be helped in many ways.

Set the stage for constructive social play. Provide sufficient equipment so that a scarcity does not provoke unprofitable conflicts. One tricycle leads to constant interference and encourages solitary play. Several tricycles leads to traffic games and turns for everyone. A wagon with a trailer and a length of chain or cord, can lead to cooperative trucking. Two swings side by side lead to companionable pumping. A rocking boat or teeter-totter calls for two or more rockers and balancers.

Do not hurry first steps in social adjustment. First adjustments to other children in school are likely to be those of watching.

Harriet, an only child aged 2.4, entered nursery school as the youngest child in the group. For two days, she spent the greater part of her mornings sitting in the tire swing, looking at all she saw going on, and apparently content with her experience. To a casual onlooker she might have apeared to be making little social progress. But on her third morning in school, she asked if Bill was there. Her mother reported that she spoke of him at home and that she was singing one of the nursery school songs at home. Harriet was taking her first steps in social adjustment at her own pace.

Shy Paul, on his second day at school in the center, was sitting on the floor with a ball in his hands. His teacher sat down a little way from him, smiled, and held out her hands for him to roll the ball to her. After a few rolls back and forth, she asked 3-year-old Mary if she would like to roll the ball with Paul. Within a few minutes, Paul was in social contact while still keeping his social distance.

Help children understand and accept others' behavior. Young children are likely to see behavior only in the light of its effect on them, not in terms of its having meaning for the person behaving.

Dicky, 2.7, had been out of school for a week with a cold. On his first morning back at school, he stood near the teacher aloof from the other children in the yard. Mary, 2.8, came over to him. She smiled in a very friendly way. He backed nearer to the teacher. Mary took his hand, which was hanging limply by his side. She began shaking it up and down. Dicky reached for the teacher, murmuring protests. His teacher said, "Mary's pleased to see you. Look, she's shaking your hand." Then, perceiving that Dicky was cold to such advances, she said to Mary, "Maybe he'd like you to give him a push on the swing," a suggestion that lead to pleasant playing together.

In another part of the yard, Jim was swinging. Peter came along and began to push him. "Don't Peter, don't push me," said Jim. When Peter continued to push him in spite of his protests, Jim leaned down and hit him. Peter looked at the teacher, who remarked, "He didn't want to be pushed this time."

In offering explanations of this sort, the teacher's purpose is to help the child see that there is some basis or motive for the behavior of others, not to indicate that the specific motive in a specific situation can always be identified and classified from observed behavior. The sort of error this subjective interpretation leads to is indicated by the small boy who said, "Daddy, you and I know that dogs which bark don't bite, but do the dogs know?"

Suggest an acceptable social approach to a child who does not seem to know how to make one. Some social approaches work and some do not. A child of older parents, who had very little experience with his own age group and was paid very little attention by the children during his first days in a nursery school, went up to some of them and said, "Play with me, I'm good, I do what I'm told." This kind of self-promotion does nothing for a child. He has to learn that to be accepted, he must make an asset, not a liability of himself. He must contribute something: a push on a wagon going up a hill or an irresistible suggestion.

A 4-year-old boy eager to join in the play of another one who had a wagonload of dirt ran up to him and said, "Hey, that's poison dirt. Let's go and put it on some flies." With these words he transformed a routine hauling operation into an exciting assignment with a lethal commodity.

Sometimes the nature of a child's contribution is a surprising one. Millie, a timid 3-year-old, came to school handicapped by a poor physical constitution and the inconvenience of glasses worn to correct strabismus. Despite teacher efforts to include Millie in children's activities, she was generally overlooked and played alone. Judge the teacher's pleasure and surprise when she saw Bill, the most sought-after boy in the group, looking raptly into Millie's face with a smile on his lips as they both stood in a patch of sunlight. After a moment of silence, he said to her with obvious pleasure, "I can see myself in your glasses." Though an extraordinary remark for a boy of any age to use in ingratiating himself with a girl of any age, its basis was clear. Millie had offered the uniquely feminine contribution of a mirror for masculine vanity.

Help children offer and accept compromise. A young child can learn to resort to arbitration rather than sabotage to achieve his ends.

John wanted very much to use a certain sieve in the sand. Bill was using it and refusing to part with it, in spite of increasing threats on John part. The teacher judged that John needed help, so she suggested, "You might get Bill the other sieve and see if he would trade with you." John welcomed the idea, and Bill was willing to make this compromise. Next time, John may be able to work out this solution by himself.

As a step in the direction of making and accepting compromise, young children frequently need help in learning to substitute verbal requests for bawls and blows. To a child who stands screaming and incoherent, clutching another child who has something he wants, try, "Tell him what you want. Maybe he will give it to you."

*Forestall undesirable social behavior by an acecptable sugges-
tion.* Priscilla sat in the sandbox putting the finishing touches
to a "cake" she had turned out from a tin mold. As she patted
it with domestic pride, two boys drew alongside. The teacher
overheard them say, "Let's bust it." She said to Priscilla, "You
have company. Maybe they'd like a piece of your cake." The
cake-busters were completely disarmed by such hospitality
and turned from their projected destruction to cake and conversation.

*Redirect unacceptable social activity in line with what the
child is seeking through his efforts.* When a child uses an unacceptable technique, his need is for an acceptable technique
rather than censure or removal from the situation. I was reminded of this when I visited a nursery school in the early
thirties. At that time it was fairly general practice to provide a
small isolation or detention area to which an offending child
could be banished for socially disruptive behavior. A pad on
the door listed each offender's name, the nature of his offense,
and the date and hour of day on which it occurred. In looking
over this chronicle of crime, I found a few offenders' names
occurring again and again. Jim, in at 10:00 for snatching, was
back at 11:00 for hitting, day after day, with slight variations
in assault tactics. Jim, in prison parlance, was a recidivist. All
he was learning was that some behaviors led to banishment,
not what he might do to keep in circulation.

Here is a more helpful approach to social disruption. Madge
was watching two boys with a wagon and tricycle tied together pushing and pulling it up the slope. This was a new
arrangement of equipment and they were having fun. She
evidently wanted to join them, but her way of doing it was to
run and snatch a pan from their wagon. One of them chased
her and took the pan. She started to do it again when the
teacher remarked, "You might help push the wagon for them."

She went up and said, "I'll help push for you." They appeared glad of her help and the three played together.

Once children grasp the general principle that they must contribute something in order to be accepted, they become fairly adroit in redirecting the social behavior of their playmates.

In a nursery school, two girls were playing lions in an abandoned aviary. A third girl ran over to join them. "Go away," roared the lions, kicking the door shut in her face. The third girl stood her ground. "You lions are hungry," she said, "I will feed you." She got some blades of grass and poked them through the netting at the ravening lions. Soon she was roaring in the cage, while the late lions were out hunting grass for her.

Set an example by your own social techniques. In her handling of situations, the teacher sets an example that the children soon imitate. Children who have attended nursery school may become very skillful in manipulating social situations by indirect suggestion, by working out compromises, and by reassuring their companions with, "You may have it as soon as I finish" or "Here is another one for you to use." Though it may be asking a lot of a teacher, her suggestions should be ones she would want a child to use in the same situation.

When a group were using the walking board, another child, Dee, tried to join them. Robert pushed him away, saying, "Get away, you can't come here." The teacher said quickly, "Yes he can," thus contradicting Robert and making Dee feel he had the backing of the teacher. Dee turned around and hit Robert who ran away. The teacher then tried to stop Dee who ran after Robert hitting him. Neither child returned to the play. More profitable support might have been given if the teacher had sugested to Dee ways of making himself acceptable, such as, "There is room for lots of people on this board," or "A long line can use this board," or "Maybe he could march behind you." These suggestion would have helped Robert to accept an addition to the group and would have indicated to Dee ways of getting into the group in a more acceptable manner than contradicting.

Devalue unacceptable behavior by ensuring that children get little satisfaction from it. Bob pulled off Tom's cap and ran and threw it over the fence. Tom started to cry. The teacher turned her attention to reasuring Tom, thus lessening the attention value of the act for Bob and strengthening Tom in his ability to meet the aggression. She said, "He is playing a joke with you. You don't need your cap just now. You are building." Another child had seen what had happened and ran and got the cap to bring it back to Tom. Bob, who had been watching to see what response he would get, took the cap from the third child, ran back to Tom, and gave him back his cap. Tom took it in a matter-of-fact way and put it on his head, for he was already absorbed in his building.

A child who is disturbing the group by disruptive activities that seem to stem from his being socially out of sorts is often helped by being directed to quiet activity by himself, like sweeping the storage shed. A short period in which few social demands are made on him often helps a child to recover his equilibrium.

Do not attempt to arbitrate all disagreements. Though children are helped by teacher's suggestions in learning to get along with each other; if these suggestions are effective, the children progressively learn to resolve their disagreements themselves. Studies of child conflicts in nursery school reveal that most conflicts are brief, occur between friends, and are reasonable well resolved by the children themselves. A teacher is concerned not so much with righting every wrong that occurs as with helping children to get along agreeably most of the time and to balance the pleasures of companionship against its occasional inevitable frustrations.

Adapt procedures to each child's need. Though membership in any group calls for accepting a few ground rules, not all children are ready for this right away.

During World War II, the 3-year-old son of an army major entered the nursery school in a khaki replica of his father's uniform and with 3 years' experience of literally following the army from post to post before settling with his maternal grandparents while his father was overseas. During his first days in nursery school, he gathered all the small trucks and cars in one corner of the sandbox and sat on them, cautiously taking one out at a time for his own use. Why? Had he had so much taken away from him in his brief post-to-post life-span that he felt a need to hang on to a few possessions? Whatever the answer, he was given time to get used to his new surroundings and to realize that what he played with today would be there for him tomorrow before any ado was made of sharing and taking turns.

Promote a community spirit of cooperative helping, sharing, and taking turns. A nursery school is a small community in which child members feel more a part when they take part in putting away toys before lunch, clearing away dishes after lunch, pouring their own juice and milk, preparing paints and washing brushes, and generally keeping the nursery school running. They also share equipment and materials. Taking turns becomes meaningful and acceptable to a child when a teacher sees that turns are fairly distributed.

Plan pleasant group-participation experiences. One way of helping children experience the pleasures of group participation is to plan some simple activities in which each child has a part, such as a cooking or gardening project or a simple field trip to a fire station or bakery.

Avoid social moralizing. Children learn from firsthand experience. They also learn that what is acceptable social behavior in the nursery school may be a little different from what is acceptable at home or in the street. Pious moralizing about what *we* or *big boys* or *big girls* do or don't do is unhelpful and untrue. It is enough for a child to learn from his own experience that some kinds of social behavior lead to good times for all and that other kinds do not, that other persons have feelings and needs like his own, that it is good to contribute and feel needed, and that there is a certain amount of sweat and tears involved in getting along with others—but it is worth it.

FROM BEING TAKEN CARE OF
TO TAKING CARE OF HIMSELF

In the twenties, when nursery schools were becoming accepted laboratories for child study on university campuses, curricular emphasis was on the three S's—sensory motor skills, socialization, and self-help. The amount of time spent in those days in the bathroom, locker room, rest room, and around the lunch table sometimes suggested that staff members might not know what to do with the children when they were not engaged in the rituals of dressing, toileting, and learning to feed themselves. Now though that more and more children under 3 years of age are being enrolled in day care centers of some sort, helping them become independent in dressing, toileting, hand-washing, and feeding themselves is a necessary part of their educational curriculum. Nor is it something that has to be thrust upon them. Most young children are eager me-doers. All of them, though, can do better with a little help.

Feeding himself

At birth an infant's response to hunger pangs is simple—he screams. When food appears, he sucks and swallows. Later, when he is being fed from a spoon or a cup, he may try to grab the spoon or the cup. This is the time to give him a spoon for himself and let him cooperate in spooning an occasional mouthful. It is also the time to give him a cup with very little milk or water in it to experiment with drinking from a cup. He has still, though, quite a way to go in learning to feed himself acceptably. This is not a simple matter of good intention for a 2-year-old. It requires mastery of several separate hand–eye–mouth and fork–spoon–food manipulations. Specifically, a child has to learn the following.

TO SEAT HIMSELF AT THE TABLE WITH HIS FEET ON THE FLOOR This is simple for a sober adult, but not so simple for a 2-year-old in a nursery school or day care center. Frequently he has to be shown or told how to pull his seat out and slide it nearer the table after he is sitting on it.

His feet are likely to stray to his neighbor's lap. Returning them quietly to the floor keeps the child's and his neighbor's attention above rather than below the table.

TO PUT ON HIS OWN BIB OR ADJUST A NAPKIN ON HIS LAP Graduation from bib to napkin is indicated when a child eats without spilling food on his chest.

TO KEEP ALL FOOD ON HIS PLATE Casual laying around of his food is likely to be a holdover from a child's high-chair days. Quietly returning his toast stick (toast cut into strips) or carrot strip from the tablecloth to his plate or an occasional reminder—"All food on your plate" or "On your plate"—leads to more organized eating.

TO CHEW WITH HIS MOUTH CLOSED Any child who *habitually* repels his eating companions with vistas of half-chewed spinach and eggs should be suspect for adenoids and commended to the attention of the school physician.

TO SWALLOW BEFORE SPEAKING   Gently remind the child who speaks from a full mouth to swallow first.

TO HOLD HIS SPOON WITH A GROWN-UP GRIP   The baby or palm grasp does not lead to the development of precision in getting food either off the plate or into the mouth. Show a child, who does not know, how to hold his spoon and quietly encourage and commend his more skillful use of it.

TO POINT THE SPOON TIP TOWARD THE MOUTH   The side presentation festoons the face with food. "This way" and a demonstration help a 2-year-old get food into his mouth instead of on his face.

TO USE A TOAST STICK, NEVER THE FINGERS TO PUSH WITH   When a child shows signs of coming to grips with his food, remind him to use his toast stick. If he has none, pass one to him.

TO HOLD THE FORK WITH A GROWN-UP GRIP FOR LIFTING FOOD, A PALM GRIP FOR CUTTING   Demonstration is more effective than recommendation.

TO DRINK FROM A GLASS WITHOUT SPILLING   Plastic, being unbreakable, is an obvious choice for small children. Handles are unnecessary.

TO POUR MILK WITHOUT SPILLING   One hand on the handle of the pitcher and the other in front to steady it make pouring practically spill-proof at any age.

TO TURN HIS HEAD FROM THE TABLE AND COVER HIS MOUTH WHEN COUGHING OR SNEEZING   Provide example, demonstration, and assistance. You may occasionally have to remind an uninhibited cougher with a look or gesture.

TO REMAIN AT THE TABLE UNTIL HE HAS FINISHED EATING   A child who rises to leave with an apple quarter in his hand can be reminded to "finish eating before you leave."

TO REPLACE DROPPED UTENSILS WITH CLEAN ONES   A basket or tray with extra utensils on the serving table simplifies replacement.

TO TAKE CARE OF MINOR TABLE ACCIDENTS   A cloth, pan, and broom in a nearby cupboard and a matter-of-fact attitude on the part of the teacher as she reminds the child "to get the cloth and wipe up" disposes of table accidents.

TO TAKE AWAY HIS LUNCH PLATE AND GET HIS DESSERT   The tedium of sitting for some time is relieved by having each child take away his own plate and pick up his dessert. The clearing-away process that requires putting plates on one tray, glasses on another, spoons and forks on another, and napkins in the waste can seems to be a simple, satisfying, classifying process for most young children. It also appears to give them a feeling of competence and independence. Other help you can give a child lies in your thoughtful choice of table appointments: chair heights that put all feet comfortably on the floor and a table height that allows free arm use. A colorful self-help bib can be replaced by a paper napkin once a child can eat without spilling. Plates with rims and such pushers as toast sticks or carrot strips help a child to get food onto a fork or a spoon. A small milk pitcher makes pouring from pitcher to glass easy. And family service, with serving dishes and spoons on the table or on a small side one, makes it possible to adjust portions to appetites.

While helping each child to acquire self-feeding skills, exercise judgment in the zeal with which you promote them. A poor eater is better left to his own devices until his appetite improves. Make whatever comment you think necessary to a child in as few words as possible and in a low gentle voice, so that a pleasant table atmosphere is not destroyed by constant reminders. First and foremost, food and drink are to be enjoyed.

Accepting and enjoying a variety of nutritionally acceptable foods

Acceptable self-feeding is not all a child can learn over lunch. He can also learn to eat and enjoy a variety of nutritionally acceptable foods without benefit of TV or radio commercials. Here, too, you can help him. In a pre-entry home visit you can ask his mother if he has any allergy or consistent food dislike. Better still, you can seek his mother's cooperation in keeping a weekend record of what he ate, when he ate it, and in what amounts—cups or tablespoons. A record of this sort gives clues to the nutritional adequacy of each child's home diet and to family food customs. Incidentally, it provides some basis for parent-group discussions of whatever problems they have in feeding their children.

The weekly menu should, of course, either be posted on the bulletin board or sent home, and any recipe asked for by a mother should be available. A teacher or dietitian can plan menus that reflect as much consideration for color, texture, taste, easy manipulation, and familiarity as for calorie, protein, mineral, and vitamin content. But to get it eaten and enjoyed—

Introduce new foods in small amounts at spaced intervals. Most young children are conservative eaters, so their first meals in the center should be planned around generally liked familiar foods. New food can then be introduced in small amounts at spaced intervals.

Combine new food with enjoyed familiar food. Combining a new food with enjoyed familiar food helps its first acceptance. In one nursery school where the children greatly enjoyed spaghetti and tomatoes, ground liver was introduced successfully by including it in this dish.

Emphasize tasting rather than eating a helping of food. This disarms the child whose announcement that he does not eat carrots is met by a quiet reply that he does not have to eat them, just taste them. Tasting is promoted to eating by the teacher's suggestion that now he has tasted them, he will soon learn to eat them as the other children do.

Offer occasional choices when the weekly menu is made up. Four-year-olds enjoy planning a lunch menu, and even the younger children like to have their suggestions for a particular dish carried out.

Serve disliked foods in very small amounts to the child who dislikes them. An older child who is learning to eat a food he dislikes is often aided by being allowed to help himself to the amount he thinks he can eat. This gives him a choice, but at the same time, ensures his becoming more accustomed to it.

Serve food in amounts the child customarily eats. In a world in which three-quarters of the population does not have enough to eat, those that have enough should not waste it. So serve the amount of food a child can eat rather than the amount you would like to see him eat. Heaping servings have the same effect on a child's appetite as on an adult's.

Let a child help himself to second servings. The opportunity to serve himself a second helping helps a child relate his intake to his appetite. It accounts for the custom of serving milk in an 8-ounce pitcher, one for each child, in nursery schools. Pouring liquid is irresistible to a young child. The only way to keep on pouring is to keep on drinking.

Sometimes a child needs help in finishing a meal. For a poor eater, the ingestion of a certain amount of food at regular intervals is a step in promoting good eating habits. Occasionally such a child may benefit from a little help in finishing his food—but only if the help is welcome.

Adapt general methods to the needs of each child. Blanche, aged 3.6, came into the nursery school just after she had recovered from whooping cough. During this period, she had brought two distracted parents almost completely under her control during her paroxysms of coughing and had even managed to regulate her diet by stating that she "was going to 'pit' up" when confronted by disliked food. At the first school lunch, she ate her first course with appetite but left her carrots. When the teacher drew her attention to them, Blanche pushed her chair back and said, "I'm going to 'pit' up." The teacher quietly suggested that Blanche do this in the toilet. She went out and returned, poked her carrots around, again announced her need for "pitting up," and was again quietly directed to the toilet. On the third trip, the teacher went along with her, raised the toilet seat, and looked expectantly at Blanche, who was confronted with the difficult situation of having a successful technique fail. To help Blanche out of this tight corner, the teacher said, in a friendly tone, "I don't believe you need to spit up. When you had the whooping cough, you were sometimes sick, but you're better now." "Oh, no," said Blanche, "I'm a very sick little girl." To hasten her return to health, the teacher said, "Yes, you *were* sick. Now you're a very fit little girl. Let's go back and take some of the carrots off your plate. You show me how many you can eat. Then you'll be ready for dessert."

Give interested children opportunities to help cook lunch and set the table. Young children like to do what they see adults doing. The sights, smells, and end results of cooking have an irresistible appeal, so why not make it possible for interested children to take some part in the preparation of lunch. Carrots grown in their own plot can be scrubbed. Peas can be podded. Apples can be stuffed and baked; so can potatoes. Meat loaf, custard, and many other standard lunch dishes are well within the culinary capability of a young child, provided he is given some supervision. All the while he can be learning something about measurement, about the effects of heat and cold on different foods, about solutions and raising agents, and the need for clean hands when cooking.

Table-setting, too, appeals to some children, and turns may be eagerly sought. This provides opportunities to count five chairs for four children and one teacher, and five place mats, each with a napkin, fork, spoon, and glass. A little simple addition and subtraction can be involved by a reminder that, since Bill is away today, there are just three children and one teacher—"How many places is that?"

In one nursery school in a part of the country in which flies were very prevalent, the opening and closing of screen doors inevitably let in a few of them. After the children all came inside and the doors were closed preparatory to setting the table, there was a brief, brisk session of fly-swatting. Swatting turns were eagerly sought by boys who apparently enjoyed combining aggression with successful aim, social approval, and sanitation.

Entering into and enjoying
the social side of eating

Sitting over food and drink with agreeable companions stimulates conversion as well as salivation. For children under 3, the social aspect of eating is subordinate to enjoying food and learning self-feeding skills. Do not stimulate conversation in this age group. For children over 3, your relaxed friendly presence will probably invite it. Aside from unobtrusive efforts to keep table talk from becoming noisy and distracting, remain an accepting, interested listener.

Your listening may be rewarded as mine was by a 4-year-old boy's revelation of his dawning awareness of the immutability of time. Dick was very partial to prune whip and always very pleased when it appeared on the table. One noon, when he was back in nursery school after a week's absence and had his favorite dessert placed in front of him, he drew a deep breath of anticipation and, holding his teacher, his friends, and his dessert in a warm glance of love, he said, "I wish I wouldn't be born for a hundred years. When you're born, after a while you die. When you die, you're dead forever." An English novelist similarly remarked concerning a farewell between friends, "In each instant of our lives we die to that instant." Dick, too, was savoring the passing of an instant in which friends and prune whip were happily combined.

Taking care of himself in the bathroom

At birth, an infant responds to pressure in his bladder or muscular sensation in his rectum by voiding or defecating regardless of attending circumstances. Before his elimination behavior is acceptable, his involuntary relaxation of the sphincter muscles concerned in voiding and defecation must be brought under voluntary control. This is not easy. In a longitudinal study of the development and behavior of over 100 children who represented a cross sample of the Berkeley population in 1928 and 1929, 35 percent of the boys and 14 percent of the girls were still wetting themselves at 2 years of age. Many 2-year-olds in a children's center may still have much to learn.

Specifically, some of them may still need to learn to associate sensations and tensions with urination or defecation and to regard them as a warning of impending urination or defecation.

They may also need to learn to delay urination until socially approved conditions are present and to arrange to get to the socially approved conditions in time.

Finally, they need to learn to unfasten buttons if necessary, flush the toilet, and wash their hands after going to the toilet.

The teaching situation in the nursery school calls for an adequate number of either junior toilet fixtures or adult fixtures made accessible to the child by steps or boxes and a child-sized seat. Equally necessary is clothing that is easily taken care of by a young child. A teacher may exert some influence on this through occasional exhibits of children's clothing and through parent–staff meetings and conferences.

Each child's level of independence can be assessed from his mother's answers to questions during a teacher's pre-entry home visit.

Assign a child with toilet problems to a teacher or assistant who can devote time to helping him. Bobby, aged 2, was brought to a nursery school associated with a public school in a congested area in a city. His mother was sick; his father was at work all day. The child was in need of the services a 9-to-4 nursery school offered. During his first week he was somewhat disturbed by the new situation and had toilet accidents at frequent intervals. In his second week an assistant was assigned to help him. On the first morning she kept a time record of his urination. When an accident occurred, Bobby was taken to the toilet, encouraged to complete emptying his bladder there, and helped into dry clothes. He gave the teacher some assistance with a short-handled mop in drying the floor. The following morning the assistant approached him a little before his urination periods of the previous morning. She said, "Toilet now, Bobby," took his hand, and went with him to the toilet. When he urinated in the toilet she said, "Fine, Bobby," and gave him a pat. On the fourth day Bobby had no accidents. Consistent help and friendly support from one person had started him on the first stage of a learning process. He had experienced the comfort of dry clothes, had been given many opportunities to associate urinating with a toilet, had been encouraged and praised when he made this association, and had become aware that the toilet was an accepted place for urination, while the playroom floor was not.

Encourage each child to develop progressive independence of regular toilet periods. Children who remain dry because a teacher reminds them or takes them to the toilet at regular periods are not required to distinguish between their sensations at a time when they need to go to the toilet and a time when they do not. When you think a child is ready to make this distinction, ask him 15 minutes in advance of a set schedule, "Toilet now?" If he says "no," say, "All right, tell me when you have to go," thus shifting the responsibility to the child, though still keeping an eye on him to prevent accidents. As soon as a child indicates that he knows when he has to go to the toilet, it is no longer necessary to keep him on a schedule. An occasional question or reminder may be all that is necessary.

Allow an older child to suffer the inconvenience of a careless accident. Occasionally an older child has accidents because he does not take the time to come indoors. In most centers or preschools, older children have no change of underwear at school. An accident, therefore, requires sitting inside while wet pants dry, a salutary experience for a child who is simply careless.

Inform a child's mother of toilet accidents. Because toilet accidents are often associated with the onset of colds or with emotional disturbances, they should be reported to a child's mother, particularly if he has previously had no difficulties with bladder control.

A young child may need help in learning to urinate or defecate in a strange bathroom. Dicky, aged 2.4, entered a summer nursery school with a morning program from 9 to 1. On his first morning, though he drank copiously and seemed in need of going to the toilet, he stood blankly in front of it. Running water and murmured suggestions from his teacher left him unmoved. After his father picked him up at noon, the teacher called his mother and learned that Dicky had gone immediately to the home toilet on arrival, with great need and great relief. Next day, though he drank even more heavily, the situation was the same. The teacher asked his mother about his toileting at home, learned that he always used a chamber pot of his own and was always taken to it by his mother. Next morning, at the teacher's suggestion, a large newspaper parcel accompanied Dicky to school. Confronted by a strange bathroom and a strange teacher, his familiar fixture redeemed the situation. It was kept at school for 2 days and, on the second noon, went home with a note to Dicky's mother which informed her that her son was now reconciled to modern plumbing facilities.

Suggestion plays a part in developing habits of bowel elimination as well as bladder control. Sometimes the teacher may be able to help a child who has developed bad habits of bowel elimination. Madge arrived late her first three mornings in nursery school. On inquiry, the teacher learned that the lateness was due to Madge's having what she called "an enemy." Her mother explained that Madge was constipated, and that constipation had run in the family for two generations, resulting in Madge's morning encounters with "the enemy"—the procedure being to sit her on the toilet for 10 minutes, with a more or less predetermined idea as to the outcome in both Madge's and her mother's minds. The teacher discussed Madge's diet with her mother, but, even after 3 days of a very laxative diet, there was no success. The teacher then decided to see what a complete change of situation would do. With the mother's approval, she told Madge that she had been late in the mornings and missing play in school because of "the enemy." She told her that tomorrow she could come to school right after breakfast and have her bowel movement in the teachers' bathroom upstairs. She was told that she would not need an enema. Next morning, Madge arrived bright and early, pleased with the distinction of sharing the teachers' bathroom. The teacher took her upstairs, gave her a bell, and told her to ring the bell as soon as she was through and not to flush the toilet. On the third step down, the bell rang loudly. When the teacher went in, Madge looked at her with great satisfaction and said, "I've done a big job!" A week's usage of the teachers' bathroom and a carry-over of the bell-ringing the first two mornings at home overcame, *at least for the time,* a tendency—inherited or not—to rely on "enemy" action.

Make hand-washing and face-washing easy and pleasurable. Since urinating or defecating calls for washing hands as well as flushing the toilet, this, too, is something in which a child may be helped to become independent. The type of washing done in a nursery school depends on the program. When the children are in school for only 3 hours, washing hands after going to the toilet or after playing with sticky materials is all that is necessary and can easily be taken care of with wash-bowls, liquid-soap containers, and paper towels. When children stay for lunch, face-washing and hair-combing call for individual towels, washcloths, combs, a child-height mirror, and some guidance from the teacher. To prevent confusion and facilitate use of the bathroom by many children during a short period, a fairly routine procedure becomes almost necessary. In one school, the following verbal statements given by the teacher explained the plan of action:

Stopper in.
Water in.
Water off.
Soap your hands.
Rinse them off.
Stopper out.
Get the cloth.
Wet the cloth.
Squeeze it out.
Wipe your face.
Hang up the cloth.
Dry face and hands.

These statements were offered *only* when a child seemed uncertain what to do next. Apparently, verbal suggestions do not disturb young children who tend to accompany many of their own activities with a statement of what they are doing. When one student teacher began "stopper in," a child forestalled any further comments from her by completing the entire series of statements. Another enlivened his father's shaving by chanting the washing routine to him.

Dressing himself and taking care of his clothes

During the second 6 months of life, a baby finds out that kicking or pulling at socks eventually removes them and that a smart tug unseats most headgear. What he learns after these initial discoveries depends on his dress and his dresser.

Share with parents information on self-help garments. Though ease in putting on and off is only one criterion in the selection of clothes, the following features are worth recommending (parents may add to these):

Two-piece underwear saves complete undressing of young children after "accidents."

One-piece underwear should have buttons firmly but loosely attached and an elastic drop seat.

Girls' pants, if buttoned, should fasten at the side with two buttons of reasonable size loosely attached. Buttonholes should be roomy.

Raglan sleeves on girls' dresses are easy to put on and allow for growth. Fitted armholes and puffed sleeves cannot be recommended on either of these scores. Front fastenings, buttons, or zippers are indicated for independent fastening.

The size and position of buttons on boys' suits govern their development of independence in managing them. Concealed buttons are too difficult for young children to fasten.

Pullover sweaters should have either a large neck-opening or a zipper front. Jackets should have front fastenings and reasonable-sized buttons.

Two-piece playsuits are more convenient for children's toileting than one-piece garments. Incidentally, they allow for growth. Zippers are the easiest fastening in stiff material.

Coveralls with a drop seat and front fastening are the simplest type of coverall garment for young children to manage. Overalls with crossed straps at the back are a difficult problem for both boys and girls at the toilet.

Drop seats in playsuits make both toileting and undressing simple for the youngest children.

Marking the front of garments with a cross helps children distinguish back from front.

Fastening gloves or mitts by a long tape to the neck of a snowsuit reminds the child to put them on and prevents their loss.

A shoehorn is an aid at all ages in putting shoes on.
A low seat makes shoe-lacing simpler.

Demonstrate and commend dressing skill. In helping a child
to dress himself, use simple consistent movements that he can
duplicate. If you are helping him learn to put on leggings, sit
beside him. This position duplicates his and makes it easier for
him to imitate your example. When he is learning to button,
let him fasten the last button, thus getting the feeling of completing the job. If he cannot get his rubbers on entirely un-
aided, encourage him to put his toes in and help him finish.
In brief, encourage him to do everything he can manage.
There are times, however, when a tired child should be helped
and not unduly burdened with the business of getting clothes
off or on. If several children are dressing or undressing in a
crowded locker room, confusion is reduced if they are reminded to put each garment away as it is taken off. No explanation is needed. Just say, "Hat away first, then your
galoshes." If interest is flagging, a comment that "Jack is
working well" or that "Bill and Jane have their hat and
sweater off and are working on their leggings" provides a little
motivation. Never resort to "Let's see who will be first."
Rather, suggest to a slow child that he keep busy or if he
disturbs others, that he undress outside the locker room by
himself.

Help children relate clothing to climate. "The ground is wet,
you will need rubbers today" or "You're getting warm John—
you could take your sweater off" are steps in this direction.

Help children learn to care for their clothes. Provide aprons
to protect clothes from sticky material and a labeled locker for
each child in which he can hang up the clothes he takes off.

"Can do" does not mean "does do." If detailed directions for
helping young children learn to do for themselves suggest an

end to helping them dress, eat acceptably, and go to the bathroom alone, this illusion must be dispelled. By the time most children have learned to do for themselves, they have learned to do many other things that are much more interesting. How do you keep self-help continuing once it has lost the charm of novelty. Having competent self-helpers demonstrate and help beginners in rolling up sleeves, washing hands, and attending to other details of their toilet, is an incentive both to the competent and to the beginners. So is taking for granted that self-help is a part of growing up.

As for occasional lapses. When did you last have your hair done for you, your nails manicured, or your "back done up"? And when did you last enjoy a meal you did not prepare, did not set table for, or clear away after?

FROM HOME AND CENTER
TO COMMUNITY

A child in any kind of center for young children learns from firsthand experience what is required for a group of people to live and get along together. In his neighborhood community, he sees a more structured specialization of effort and contribution. What he can see, apart from family outings, depends on what is to be seen within about a three-block radius of his center.

Survey community facilities within three blocks of the children's center. Regardless of how restricted to housing units a neighborhood may be, a walk around the block will reveal, at least, a fire hydrant, a fire alarm box, a mailbox, a manhole, a street light, street markings, traffic signs, overhead electric light and telephone wires, as well as trucks, delivery vans, and buses in transit. Specialized activities of community members may also be represented by:

People who produce goods—bakery, dairy, factory workers.

People who distribute these goods—retail store, delivery workers.

People who produce services—teachers, shoemakers, dry cleaners, doctors, cooks, barbers.

People who maintain a system of exchange—bank tellers.

People involved in transportation and communication—bus drivers and switchboard operators.

People involved in a variety of construction activities—carpenters, welders, plumbers, electricians.

People engaged in governing activities—maintaining law and order (police), ensuring community health and safety (street cleaners), and dispatching mail (postmen).

Many children's centers are in a building in which other activities are going on. What is more natural than children wishing to know something about these activities and so feel more at home in their center? Moreover, since tradesmen and servicemen are sometimes around the center premises, why not have them occasionally stop long enough to give the children some idea of what they do?

Plan friendly, informing encounters with visiting tradesmen and servicemen. Most adults enjoy talking with young children and showing them what they do and answering their questions. The milkman delivering the milk, the garbage man, the fireman making a routine check on fire extinguishers, the school nurse and doctor on their periodic visits may be willing to take a few minutes to show the children some of the things they do.

Develop community experiences from children's activities and interests. Some 4-year-olds were working at the clay table. One of the girls rolled a round ball. "This is a head for a doll," she said. "I'll make you a body," offered one of the boys. Soon head, arms, and limbs were assembled, but then difficulties arose in getting the doll together. While they were working, the teacher asked them if they would like to see a factory where dolls were made. The children were delighted at the prospect. They wanted to know where it was, whose factory it was, and what sort of dolls were made. The teacher told them the factory was in a small building owned by Mr. Swenson, who had 10 women and 1 man working with him. Next day Mr. Swenson met them at the door of the factory. He showed them the barrels of powdered clay and told them that some of it came from England. He explained that he got it from there because it baked so hard and strong. Then he showed the children the molds for the dolls' heads, bodies, arms, and legs. In a big room lighted with windows, women were at work dusting off the arms and bodies that had been baked the day before. They talked with the children, and Mr. Swenson showed them how they wiped off the parts. In another room, a small motor connected by belts with several large mixers furnished the power for the working and mixing of the clay. The man working there showed the children the glaze he painted on the dolls before they were baked. He showed them a piece of glazed and unglazed pottery, and they agreed that the glazed was prettier. Then Mr. Swenson took them to see where the dolls were baked. The children got inside to see how big the kiln was while Mr. Swenson showed them how the molds were made and gave them a few discarded ones to take back and try themselves with their own clay. The teacher asked Mr. Swenson where he sold his dolls. He told her the towns they went to and the name of a local store that carried them. The teacher said they would like to buy two dolls for the children's houseplay and would get them from the store. One of the children asked why she did not buy them from Mr. Swenson. The teacher explained that Mr. Swenson sold them only to stores and that when people wanted to buy one or two, they went to the store to buy them. She said that in the factory, everyone was busy making dolls and had no time or place to sell them. "Shops and stores," she told them, "are on main streets and the people working in them spend all day selling and wrapping up and taking the money for the things bought there." The teacher thanked Mr. Swenson for giving his time to show them around and told him how much they had all enjoyed it. The children drove home with their molds tightly clasped, well pleased with their first glimpse of industry and production.

Other community experiences developed from children's activities and interests, which they seemed to enjoy, were the following:

A visit to the fireboats at the San Francisco pier, which followed a child's question about how fires were put out on ships.

A visit to a bakery after the children had made a loaf of bread themselves.

A visit to a dairy after they had made both butter and ice cream themselves.

A trip to the grocery to get a pumpkin for Halloween.

A trip to the library to exchange some books.

A visit to a branch post office to mail some Valentine cards they had made.

A trip to the printing department of the university press after the 4-year-olds had used some handstamps and put together a picture book of trucks cut out of magazines.

A visit to a railway station and to the yacht harbor after stories about trains and ships.

A visit to a church to see and hear the organ. (An assistant teacher's husband was the church organist.)

Create opportunities for children to be customers, consumers, and producers. The 4-year-olds were very anxious to build a house. The teacher asked them what sort of house they wanted. For many afternoons they talked of its size, its windows, its doors, its roof, and how it would be made. They went to see a new building being put up on the campus. Their urge to build increased with every shovel of dirt they saw the steam shovel raise and every upright they saw driven into position. They listened eagerly to stories of house-building and pored over the story book pictures. Finally, when their plans had been reduced to a workable level, the teacher brought out a yardstick and they helped her measure while she wrote down the length and size of lumber they would need for the walls, the posts for the corners, and the number of shingles. They all went to the lumberyard to do the ordering and swelled with importance when their own lumber, cut to order was delivered next day. Busy as beavers, they helped to make the holes, fit in the uprights, and pour the cement for a firm foundation. For days they patiently hammered and fitted until the house was ready for staining. Then the teacher suggested that they wear their overalls to help with the staining. At last, complete with window boxes and a street number, they had their house ready to play in, to furnish, and to possess.

Use all naturally occurring opportunities to acquaint children with the contributions of producers of services. The student teacher of the 4-year-olds had been absent for 4 days because of an emergency appendectomy. The children asked about her each day and were told that she was sick, that she was in the university hospital, and that the doctors and nurses were helping to make her well again. The substitute teacher suggested that the children might like to write her a letter. Together the children assembled a page of news items, inquiries as to the exact nature of her condition, and remarks on their own past illnesses. Then they set out to deliver the letter in person to the hospital, which was only a block away. When there, they stood tiptoe to look over the information desk and see that the letter was safely delivered to the secretary. They asked who the man was who was wheeling the stretcher on the casters, and were told that he was an orderly, that he helped the doctors and the nurses to move beds and stretchers and the wagons with food on them. As the elevator opened to let off a white-coated doctor, one of the girls said, "My daddy's a doctor. He makes sick people well." "Yes," said the teacher, "doctors and nurses both help to make sick people well, the orderlies and maids help to make the hospital clean and comfortable, and the cooks in the kitchen cook the meals. They all help."

Consider the educational content of a community experience before undertaking it. If children are making something to send home, like a Valentine's or Mother's Day card, they can hardly help learning something about the postal system. But will they learn all they could? They could learn:

Their home and school street addresses.

That all envelopes must have the right (for weight) stamp pasted in the right place (upper right-hand corner).

That air mail envelopes have colored edges or markings.

That the postmark has the date the letter was mailed.

That the zip-code numbers tell the "sorter" the state, town, and street a letter is going to.

That the mailbox has on it the times of day the mail is picked up.

That in a post office, different workers do different things— weigh letters and parcels; stamp how they are to be handled (air mail, fragile); sell stamps; sort and cancel mail; pick it up from mailboxes; deliver it; and take it by vans to airports, docks, and railway stations.

To ensure selective direction of children's attention in a trip to the post office, you will need to look over the post office in advance.

Make a survey trip before any trip with children. In a survey trip, you can plan such practical details as where to park if car transportation is used, and you can gauge what can be seen from a child's height and in what order what is seen will be most meaningful. You can also give whomever you plan to visit some idea of how long your visit will be, how many children you are bringing, and their ages and interests.

Provide recall and integration of what was seen, heard, and done in a community experience. When children have had a visit to a post office, what more natural than to make some occasion for sending each of them a card through the mail? What more natural, too, than to help them—if they seem interested—in assembling a "post office" with a counter, mailbag, mailman's hat, and child-made stamps, envelopes, and scales so that they can play what they know? Help them, too, by pinning up on a bulletin board a simple pictorial map, a calendar, envelopes of different kinds with canceled stamps, a stamp with the number of cents it costs pasted alongside, and some pictures of mail vans, mailmen, post offices, mail cars, and mail being loaded on ships and planes.

Help children get some sense of the value of each worker's contribution. In all of their community experiences, children can get some sense of the value of each worker's contribution regardless of what the work is. Help them learn to call the custodian, the cook, the doctor, the nurse, and whomever they encounter by his or her title. When any worker has taken time to show or tell them what he does, help the children to send a note of thanks dictated in their own words.

Give children examples and experience in responsible, courteous citizenship. In a good nursery school, a child learns through doing what is involved in being a contributing, considerate member of a small community. As he goes out on field trips, he can learn to show some of the same cooperation and consideration in the larger adult community. Specifically, when he is taken to a park, he can learn to look at flowers, not pick them. If he has a picnic snack, he can learn to tidy up and make use of litter bins. When he crosses a street, he can learn to heed the traffic signal and stay on the sidewalk, not run into or crowd passersby. Courteousness and consideration are learned, not inborn. Without them, life in any community is less pleasant.

Several years ago I was walking up a Berkeley street behind one of the wispy little old ladies so frequently seen in Berkeley during its pleasant preprotest years. It was noon, and as we neared a fraternity house, a surge of fraternity brothers spilled onto the sidewalk, talking, laughing, and scuffling. The wispy old lady was literally swept into the street. As she tried to steady herself, one of the brothers saw her. Without changing pace or position, he said perfunctorily, "I'm sorry." And then, minding his manners, added, "Jesus, I'm sorry!" The university fraternity was next door to the university nursery school. The nursery school children could, I think, have shown the brothers a more considerate way of sharing the sidewalk.

FROM "ME" TO "WHO AM I?"

In a child's discovery of the physical world, of nature and art, of the power of speech, of likeness and difference, of causality and probability, and of human relationships, he in some sense discovers himself. This ongoing discovery appears to begin in the first 6 months of life, when a baby contemplates and plays with his hands and later plays with his toes, thereby presumably getting some notion of the extent of his person. A test item for an 18-month-old child in the Gesell Developmental Schedules is to point to his nose, eyes, and hair, thus showing awareness of some of his anatomical parts. Most children at this age also answer to their names.

By the time a child enters a children's center at 2 years of age, much of what he has discovered about himself mirrors his parents' and siblings' opinion of him. In his years in the center, he continues to be influenced by what his teachers and child companions help him to see in himself.

How can he be helped in this ongoing process of finding out who he is? Who is he?

A young child is a biological organism. Studies of children's anger and fear support popular belief that a young child who is feeling poorly feels vulnerable and less able to cope with disturbing circumstances. Other studies suggest that his physical well-being is basic to his effective mental and social functioning and to his emotional buoyancy. Head Start revealed a surprising number of handicapping health defects in young children in poor economic circumstances. For any young child in such circumstances, medical and dental care and nutritional supplements are essential features of an effective educational program. For all children, a health-promoting daily regime is equally essential.

A young child is also a reacting organism. Some children are more reactive than others. Marked reactivity takes a toll of nervous energy which is then not available for other purposes. Sluggish reactivity may make a child less sensitive to his surroundings, less open to living. The overreactive are helped by calm, consistent, predictable procedures; the sluggish by stimulating their curiosity and interest.

A young child is what he can do. In a child's doing, achieving, and mastering lies the source of much of his confidence as well as competence. This is why it is necessary to give each child a chance to exercise and develop *all* the skills of which he is capable. In this exercise, what is important is not to prepare him to meet or surpass some performance standard but to help him find out what he can do, what he likes to do and does well, and what is worth doing. In an English film, *The Loneliness of the Long-Distance Runner*, a teen-ager committed to a rural detention center because of juvenile delinquency in a slum neighborhood is given the opportunity and freedom to practice cross-country running. This opportunity is given him so that he can establish a competitive record for the center and confirm a tweedy sponsor's faith in sportsmanship and all that. On the day of the race, as he jogs over the countryside he knows so well from his lonely practice runs, the runner has time for bitter reflection. In the homestretch, far in advance of all competitors, he throws the race.

This film has, I think, implications for planning compensatory education programs for disadvantaged young children. It is not enough to ensure that they know their right hand from their left and can speak in a way that helps them fit into a standard kindergarten program. Nor is it enough to prove the worth of one educational method over that of others. The real worth of any program of this sort lies in what it does for each child's sense of his own worth.

A young child is what he can sense. We live in a motoric era. We deface the landscape to get rapidly from one part of it to another. We are for doing and acting, rather than sensing. Most of us spend our lives among sights and sounds that displease us. Multisensory bombardment and a level of noise that dulls our hearing acuity are an inescapable part of our environmental pollution. Within a center for young children, it is a challenge to create an environment that invites and rewards sentience.

A young child is what he can understand. A child lives in a world of his own discovery and understanding. The riches of this world are the limits of his ability to discover and understand. His home and parents, his nursery school, and his teachers can offer the means whereby his discovery and growth of understanding can be promoted.

A young child is what he can imagine. A child can invent his own world. Sometimes the world of his invention takes shape in his use of crayons and paints, blocks and clay, or in his dramatic play. He needs, therefore, a variety of media to find the one that most stimulates his urge to innovate. Most of all, he needs companions his own age who can share his fantasy in ways impossible to an adult. But he also needs adults who accept his fantasy in an "I too, make-believe spirit" and who enjoy with him the humor of his imaginings.

A young child is what he can feel. A friend of mine who is a philosopher is in the habit of taking his grandson for a walk everyday to local points of interest. When the grandson was 2, he often tired after seeing the train go by or the plane come down and asked to be carried. One day when he was 1 1/2 years older and heavier, he asked to be carried. His grandfather, who was also 1 1/2 years older and not in as good carrying form, said, "You're a big boy now. You can walk." The little chap looked at him. "I know I'm a big boy," he said, "but I feel like a little boy."

A young child feels as well as imagines and what he feels is not scaled to his size. Because his feelings are so naked, there is a tendency on the part of adults to deny their existence as well as their expression. "You're all right" and "You're a big boy" are standard adult devices for denying a child's feelings. So are books and stories in which children his age are always calm, cheerful, and conforming, never cross, cruel, or conceited. To a child beset by occasional black moods and dirty deeds, they offer no reassurance about the universality of his condition. He needs help in accepting his feelings without guilt or shame, while modifying their expression in socially acceptable ways. How can he know what others feel if he is not free to feel himself?

He needs help, too, in relating his feelings to the realities of their source if he is not to go through life making emotional mountains out of molehill circumstances.

I was recently at a cocktail party where the 4-year-old son of the house was passing around a plate of hors d'oeuvres. Overcome by his responsibilities and the attention he was attracting, he dropped the plate—a handsome Chinese one. This was shattering for the boy as well as the plate. He burst into tears, but, looking down, he stopped in midsob. "Only two bits," he said, apparently feeling that a two-bit break did not merit a many-bit lament.

A young child is a boy or a girl. Even in this period of changing sex roles, young children are expected to have some sex-role identification. This may be harder for boys than girls because they spend so much of their time with women. Male child-center assistants, male volunteers, and male visitors are, therefore, assets in any center for young children.

A young child is a member of his peer group. In constant association with adults, a young child might well feel inadequate and dependent. With his age peers, he gets a truer picture of what it means to be a 3-year-old. In their behavior he finds validation, if not self-congratulation, for his own. He also savors friendship. Friendship, though, has its thorns.

With young companions who are more self-centered and capricious than his parents, a young child experiences being spurned as well as sought after, blamed as well as praised, and defeated as well as successful, often in the course of minutes. Given the support of a perceptive parent or teacher, he can develop the ability to handle these sudden reverses and conflicting emotions. He can balance his frustrations against his fulfillments and his successes against his failures.

He can learn to take it without feeling resentful or sorry for himself.

A young child is a member of a family. A proud father looking at his son sometimes asks, "Who's dad's boy?" In the enduring love of fond and wise parents, and in the consistency of their mild control, a young child can feel the security that comes of belonging, of being cherished and guarded. In the many ways that fond parents show their child they need him as much as he needs them, and the opportunities they give him to help them, he can get a feeling of his worth. He is wanted and valued. The rightness of what he does is validated by their approval. He can balance the resentment of their restrictions against the security of their continuing support.

Not all parents are fond and wise, nor do they all give their child mild, consistent control and a sense of his social worth. They are, though, the main source of a young child's security, so a teacher must be careful not to say or do what a young child might regard as a criticism or negation of the worth of his home and family.

During the blitz of Britain in World War II, the most upsetting feature of billeting slum children in the relative safety of country homes was their host parents' well-intentioned but emotionally devastating act of burning the ragged, verminous clothes that were the children's only tangible link with their mums.

A young child is a member of a social subgroup. In the United States we are very group oriented. We group and tend to segregate on the basis of age; occupation; education; religious and political affiliation; civic, cultural, and athletic interests; ethnic origin; and social status. We are teen-agers, students, senior citizens, eggheads, hard hats, liberals, conservatives, disadvantaged, third world, black and beautiful, middle class, or jet set. We tend to identify individuals with the group to which we think they belong and with the characteristics and life-style we think go with the group, and we are more at home with what we think is our own group life-style. This poses a problem for a teacher of children belonging to a group different from what she thinks is her own. If she is not to take from a child whatever assets he has in being a member of his group, she must become group free, able to accept all groups, to enjoy their diversity, and to regard them as members of the human family.

A young child can make some choices. In a child's choices is the promise of his becoming. In his accepting the disadvantages as well as the advantages of his choices is the promise of his maturity. This is what makes free-play periods at home or in a nursery school so valuable. A child chooses what materials he will use, how long he will stay with them, and (within limits of their constructive use) what he will do with them. He feels the authority and responsibility of his choices. Giving a young child progressive opportunity to make the choices of which he is capable is a part of his education and the path to his self-determination. What is education but the education of a child's choices?

4

WHAT
DO THEY LEARN?

WHAT A YOUNG CHILD HAS LEARNED IS EVIDENT IN WHAT HE DOES,
says, understands, and shows signs of feeling. Below are a
few performances listed under each of the 17 areas of learning that may help give you some idea of some of the things
a 4- or 5-year-old child may have learned at the children's
center and at home.

Keep a dittoed list for each child, with his name at the top,
and check off what he can do whenever you notice him doing
it. You may also want to set aside a day for each child on
which he is given opportunities to try what you may not have
seen him attempt. Do not, though, make him aware of what
you are checking, lest he become anxious and feel he *should*
be able to do what he cannot. *This is not a test* on which you
try to get a score from each child. It is just a means of giving
you some idea of what each child can say, do, or understand.

Several of the performances are either the same as or similar to ones in such tests as the Metropolitan Readiness, the
Vineland Social Maturity Test, the Illinois Test of Psycho-
linguistic Abilities, the Wechsler Intelligence Scale for Children, the Peabody Picture Test, and the Stanford-Binet.

Because a child's performance on these tests gives *some* indication of how he will get along in a standard first grade, his performance on some of the items I have listed *may* do the same. You may also want to jot down under each of the 17 headings other things you have seen a child do, say, or understand that seem to you to represent a learning progression. And you may find all of this helpful in your weekly staff discussion of each child's progress.

A LEARNING CHECKLIST

FROM SENSING AND SORTING TO SYMBOLIZING

A. Can the child:

1. pick out a ball and a block in a feeling box when asked or when shown "one like this" (holding up a smaller model of ball and block)?
2. match or sort wooden lowercase letters *o, c,* and *e,* and the letters *o, c,* and *e,* each printed on a separate card?
3. match or sort the geometric forms ○ □ △?
4. fit together a puzzle of three pieces, five pieces, more than five pieces?

B. What does the child seem particularly responsive to: the sight (color or shape), sound, smell, taste, or feel of things? (Underline)

FROM SPONTANEOUS TO CONTROLLED, COORDINATED, SELF-DIRECTED, AND IMITATIVE MOVEMENT

A. Can the child:

1. throw a ball into a can at 3 feet or further away?
2. stay between lines in tracing a letter such as S?
3. hold up his right or left hand?
4. understand position and direction words when asked to move something? (Underline)

up	before	near	from
down	behind	nearer	in front of
on	between	far	round and round
over	in	farther	next to
under	out	to	

B. Is he markedly hyperactive (never still) —— sluggish —— neither ——?

C. Is he right- or left-handed when crayoning?

FROM BABBLING TO LANGUAGE

A. Can the child:
1. use sentences of five or more words?
2. correctly use plurals for foot, hand, man, and tooth?
3. correctly use *almost, always, sometimes, only, because, if, or,* and *except*? (Underline)
4. correctly use the past and future tenses of the verbs to *be,* to *have,* and to *do*?
5. respond to "Mr. X is mending the wagon. Here he comes. The wagon is ———"?

B. List any articulation defects and the most memorable remark you have heard the child make.

FROM DECODING GRAPHIC SYMBOLS TO READING

A. Can the child:
1. arrange a set of Sequees or "read" a pictograph?
2. tell what is missing in incomplete drawings of objects familiar to him?
3. tell page by page, word by word, the story in a favorite picture book?
4. recognize some letters (how many)?
5. recognize some words (how many)?

B. Does he like books and stories and have his own library card?

FROM SCRIBBLING TO WRITING

A. Can the child:
1. use a kindergarten pencil?
2. copy a circle and a square?
3. make his initials?
4. print his first name?

B. Has he ever asked you to show him how to make a letter?

FROM EXPERIENCING
TO PROCESSING INFORMATION

A. Can the child:

1. sort and use class names for fruits, vegetables, clothes, and furniture?
2. count out five of anything?
3. sort and match cards with four pictured objects, no matter how arranged?
4. seriate five rods in size order and tell you which is the longer of two rods?
5. put together those that are the same in a collection of big and small, white and red, beads?

B. How does this child tend to sort out what is the same—with a quick decision or with reflective analysis?

FROM MAGIC TO NATURAL PHENOMENA

A. Can the child:
1. pick out what is used (among a thermometer, scales, and yardstick) to find how warm, how heavy, or how long something is?
2. show and tell what happens when a pebble, ball, piece of ice, lump of sugar, or scoop of paint are put into a jar of water?
3. explain what is silly about a line drawing of two big boys on one end of a teeter-totter being balanced by a very small boy on the other end?
4. with a magnet, find out what is made of iron? with a balance, find out which is heavier—a jar of absorbent cotton or one of pebbles?

FROM BIRDS AND BERRIES
TO ORGANISMS AND ECOSYSTEMS

A. Can the child:
1. tell what flies, what swims, what crawls, what runs on four legs, what animal feels warm, what one feels cold?
2. tell where milk comes from?
3. tell what plants need to make them grow?
4. tell where several animal species live and what they eat?

B. Has the child ever brought in or told you about an animal or plant he saw?

FROM LINES, DAUBS, AND SMEARS TO PICTURES

1. What art medium does the child use most?

2. Can he match and name *red, blue, yellow, orange, green, purple*?

3. What is characteristic in his use of color, line, design, and representation?

4. What does he include when he draws a man?

B. Does he often, occasionally, or very rarely draw or paint? Does he experiment or repeat in using art media?

FROM MAKING THINGS TO USING TOOLS AND DEVELOPING HANDICRAFT SKILLS

A. Can the child use a hammer, saw, vice, scissors, stapler?

B. Has he ever made something entirely of his own devising?

FROM BOUNCING TO DANCING

A. Can the child:

1. clap out a marked rhythm in music?

2. imitate a rhythmic tattoo on a drum?

3. bounce in time to music with marked rhythm?

B. Does he seem to enjoy rhythmic activity?

FROM LALLING TO SINGING

A. Can the child:

1. sing back to you the note you sang to him?

2. sing back on a descending scale interval?

3. sing in tune a few bars of a simple song?

B. Does he sing spontaneously as he plays and seem eager to join in group song?

FROM HEARING MUSIC TO LISTENING TO IT

A. Can the child:

1. recognize the sound of a piano, recorder, autoharp, or any other three instruments?

2. tell you if a sound like a cow's moo, a train's whistle, and so on, goes up, comes down, or stays the same?

3. ask for a piece of music by name or by singing or humming a bar or two?

4. recognize any melodies?

B. Does he ask for music to listen to?

FROM AWARENESS OF OTHERS
TO GETTING ALONG WITH THEM

1. Have you heard the child express pleasure in another's achievement or sympathize with another's misfortune?
2. Have you heard the child make a contribution of interest, help, encouragement, or ideas to his child companions?
3. Have you heard the child offer and accept a compromise when he and another child both wanted the same thing?
4. Does the child take turns without monopolizing more often than not?
5. Does the child accept group rules and sometimes quote them?

FROM BEING TAKEN CARE OF TO TAKING CARE OF HIMSELF

A. Can the child:
   1. use a fork to feed himself?
   2. pour milk from a 12-ounce pitcher without spilling?
   3. stack dishes after lunch?
   4. button, snap, zip, lace, tie laces?
   5. put on socks and shoes?
   6. go to the toilet by himself and remember to flush it?
   7. wash and dry his hands?

B. Does he like to help others as well as take care of himself?

FROM HOME AND CENTER TO COMMUNITY

1. Does the child know his street address and number, the town and state he lives in, and the street address of his school?
2. Does the child know the purpose of the following: mailbox, hydrant, manhole, street sign, house number, traffic light, overhead wire, service station?[1] (Underline)
3. Has the child some idea of what is done by the mailman, policeman, garbage man, fireman, bus driver, grocer, doctor, teacher, street cleaner, nurse?[2]
4. Does the child know why stamps are put on envelopes before mailing?

[1]Only applicable for a child living in a community where he sees these.
[2]See footnote 1.

FROM "ME" TO "WHO AM I?"

1. What does the child enjoy most and do best?
2. Which of the following adjectives describe the child?

buoyant	independent	resourceful	healthy
imaginative	responsive	curious	interesting
reflective	cooperative	happy	poised
competent	industrious	interested	

3. Does he know his name, age, both day and month; street address; and the names of members of his family?

5
TEACHING: WHAT IS IT?

WHAT A YOUNG CHILD CAN LEARN AND WHAT HE DOES LEARN depend in part on what he is taught, on how he is taught, and when. What is teaching?

A famous actor, asked what he did in acting, said he talked loud enough for everyone to hear and didn't bump into things. Teaching, like acting, is a creative art. No one can tell another how to teach, but a teacher with some experience can offer a few simple suggestions of a "be-a-good-model-and-praise-progress" sort that may help a beginner to develop his or her own teaching style.

Though teaching is an art, it is probably clear from the preceding pages that it draws on the findings of the behavioral sciences. The art is in applying these findings appropriately. It is also in bringing what you know of what is known within the grasp of a particular learner's mind. Because a young child is a laboratory rather than a lecture student, teaching him is largely a matter of providing him with materials and activities in such a way that he can learn from his own experience and generalize in his own words. Some ways of helping him do this are suggested in the sections that follow: on "Getting to Know Each Child," "Getting to Know What to Say," and "Using Educational Strategies Selectively and Adaptively."

GETTING TO KNOW
EACH CHILD

As Anna in the *King of Siam* makes lyrically clear, to teach a child, you must get to know him.

How do you get to know a young child—suppositious though such knowing may be. For that matter, how do you get to know anyone of any age. By being with him, by looking at what he does, listening to what he says, and sharing experiences with him, by being yourself and leaving him free to be himself. What you look at, what you listen to, and what kinds of experience you share naturally affect what you get to know.

Look, listen, and share experiences. Here is a glimpse of how an unusual teacher got to know some school-age children. In 1859 Tolstoy opened a free school for peasant children to which, for 3 years, he gave his life and his "passionate affection." Disregarding prevailing rigid methods of teaching, he created a free, joyous atmosphere in which he shared with the children, to the limits of their desires and capacities to understand and enjoy, what he knew of literature and history, art and music, science and social philosophy, as well as the basics of reading, writing and arithmetic. When the children wearied, he would challenge them to race him outdoors to play. Fifty years later, one of the peasants[1] said of his school days:

Hours passed like minutes. If life were always as gay no one would ever notice it go by. . . . We were unhappy without the Count and he was unhappy without us.

[1] Tolstoy's favorite pupil who he referred to in his writing as Fédka.

The Count shared, too, his own passion for catching life in words. In a lesson on Russian language, he suggested that the children write a story to illustrate a Russian proverb. "Write it yourself," the children said. But they looked over his shoulder. They didn't like what he was writing. So they tried to help him, and as they sensed the excitement of the creative process, they took over entirely, each in his own way.

"Sémka," Tolstoy wrote, "seemed to see and describe [what] was before his eyes"—"The stiff bast shoes of the old soldier he was writing about and how the mud oozed from them as they thawed. Fédka, to the contrary, saw only the details which stirred in him the feelings he tried to evoke." He created the old woman, who growled as, at the command of her husband, she took off the soldier's bast shoes, and the pitiful groan of the old man as he muttered through his teeth, "Softly Motherkin, I have sores here."[2]

Who but Tolstoy could have sensed in Fédka, a peasant boy with a bare knowledge of reading, what he was so sensitive to himself—the art of expressing thought and feeling in words.

Get to know the child's life setting. What the children said and did in his school was not all that Tolstoy got to know about them. He often walked home with them at night, seeing through the lighted windows of the peasant houses, the life within and each child's reunion with his family. Throughout his life, Tolstoy was as passionately, if inconsistently involved in the life and lot of the peasants as he was for a few years with the education of their children. But then, how can anyone understand what a child does without some idea of how he is done by? Could Ann Sullivan have been as effective in teaching her blind and deaf pupil, Helen Keller, had she not lived with her in her home, sharing the storms and frustration a child with such a handicap creates and endures?

[2]Leo Tolstoy, *Tolstoy on education,* translated from the Russian (*Pedagogical articles 1862*) by Leo Wiener (Chicago: University of Chicago Press, 1967), p. 195. Introduction © 1967 by The University of Chicago.

So, before a young child leaves his home and mother to go to his first school, the place for him to meet his first teacher for the first time is in his home, not in her school. Then, in nursery school he has a continuing link with home in a teacher who knows where he lives, knows his mother and father and how they speak to him and play with him, knows his brothers and sisters, his pets and his toys, knows what he sees when he looks out his window or down his street. His world is not fractured or fragmented by going to school. And his teacher is better able to see him whole: a part of the life setting he can change and be changed by.

Expecting rather than accepting behavior is on obstacle to knowing. Parents, too, have advantages in getting to know their children. Most can and do spend considerable time and share many experiences with each of them. Few children, though, speak as rapturously of their hours with their parents as the peasant did of his with Tolstoy. This may be because parents are often hindered in getting to know their child by what they expect. A study of problem behavior in "planned for" children revealed that some parents planned not for *a* child but for a *particular type* of child. As a result, they were unable to reconcile the child of their conception with the child of their frustrated plans. What they got to know about him was that he was not what they expected, and that, therefore, something must be wrong—with the child.

Focus on developmental performances. Nursery school and kindergarten teachers also have expectations about a young child's behavior. They have, though the advantage, if their professional training has been adequate, of being able to accept a range of differences in different children. They are also probably acquainted with some of the standardized tests developed to explore and compare young children's performance at different ages in activities that seem basic in their mental development. And this gives them one kind of focus on some of the things a child can do, say, and understand. What are some of these performances an informed teacher is alerted to?

Imitating movements like waving bye-bye in his first year of life; copying a three-block building in his second year; or a circle, cross, square triangle, or diamond in later years.
Sorting out or matching what looks the same or different.
Fitting a piece of a puzzle into the space it fits.
Seeing what is missing when one of four objects is taken from a set while he is not looking.

These four performances give some clue to what a child notices, how he sorts out or classifies what he sees, and how ready and interested he may be to see differences in such symbols as letters and figures.

Handing over four or five of whatever is to hand and pointing to the biggest, middle-sized, or smallest of three blocks suggests that a child has progressed from a one to many way of looking at things and is beginning to think of them in a small-to-big order—a helpful preliminary to counting and recognizing what comes after five or six.
Solving simple problems, such as what must you do when you are thirsty, shows at least a beginning in understanding cause and effect.
Using and understanding words, not just those that tell what is happening but when, where, how often, and why is another clue to his level of thinking.
Suggesting novel ways of using some familiar household piece, such as a table—to hide under as well as sit up to, to turn upside down for a boat, and the like—reveals imagination.

Find out what a child is praised or punished for. Different children are rewarded or punished for different doings at home. Because attitudes are as important as aptitudes in learning, a teacher needs to have some idea of what a child is encouraged in or discouraged from doing at home. How can she find this out? She can listen to what children say they like to do, what is fun to do, what they say is good or bad. After a story about a child's or an animal's doing, she can ask casually, "Do you think that was a good thing to do?"

A teacher can also get some idea of what children are praised or rebuked for from their parents comments. What they ask her or tell her about their child and what they say to him when they leave or call for him often reveal what they value in his behavior. Moreover, since all young-child groups have some kind of parent get-together and since most parents are eager to talk over their children and their parental lot, a group discussion might get underway with, "What did your Bill or Mary do last week that pleased you?" "How did you let him know you were pleased?" "What did he do that made you mad?" "How did you let him know that you didn't like what he did?" What is revealed to parents as well as to the teacher in an interchange of this sort can pave the way for discussing different ways of thinking about, encouraging, or discouraging different kinds of behavior.

Any focus, though, that is restricted to selected performances and attitudes may restrict rather than extend what a teacher gets to know. It also may not help her much in finding out *how a child gets to know*. But if she looks, listens, seems interested but not interfering, a child sometimes offers a brief revealing glimpse of his private world.

Try to see it his way. In a university nursery school, two 3-year-olds were playing horses. A little girl was offering her horse some cereal shaken from a packet into a small bowl. While it is true that horses eat cereal, they don't eat bowl-sized portions, nor are they served brands recommended in television commercials. So at story time I asked the children if they would like to see the horses on the university farm and that afternoon made a preliminary visit to ensure their seeing as much as I thought they would be interested in and could understand. Next morning, we arrived under a drizzling sky to find the horses in their barn stalls and the elderly stableman pottering around looking after them. The children were warmly welcomed and were soon completely at home, stroking the star on Prince's forehead, offering wisps of straw within safe distance of munching jaws, inspecting and commenting on all that the stable offered in sights, smells, sounds, and feels of leather, horsehair, hay, and hide. All the while, the stableman rambled on in a reminiscent, affectionate vein, minding the time when Bessie kicked out two slats of her stall and Duke ran away. In this warm and friendly atmosphere of shared past experience, a 4-year-old boy studied the stableman thoughtfully. As we turned to go, he took my hand and whispered, "Is he the horses' father?"

"Mr. Grimes," I told him, as we walked slowly back to the nursery school "looks after the horses *like* a father. He is called a stableman because looking after horses is what a stableman does. He keeps the stable clean and warm when it is wet and cold. He gives the horses fresh water to drink, he fills their bins with corn and straw, he brushes their coats when they get dusty, puts their harness on when they go out to work, and takes it off and lets them out in the paddock when their work is done. He talks to them and pats them because he likes them." "I would like to be a stableman," one of the listeners broke in. Time enough later to provide the experiences that may give some clue to the biological concept of a male begetter of his species.

In another nursery school in which parents prided themselves on giving their children sex information, asked for or not, 3-year-old Sue commented on the big stomach of her mother's pregnant friend. Her mother explained that her friend was going to have a baby and was carrying the baby inside her body. "Don't you remember," she reminded, "I told you I carried you inside my body before you were born?"

Sue gave her mother a sly, secret smile. "Did you know," she asked, "that I used to come out at night and play around and then creep back?" What are words and explanations to a child who does not have the experience to make them meaningful?

What a child learns changes him. So getting to know a child is not a once-and-forever undertaking. It is an ongoing, looking, listening, sharing, sensing, and changing focus with, once in a while a brief revealing glimpse to remind us how hard it is for an adult to "become as a child."

GETTING TO KNOW
WHAT TO SAY

Though teaching is an art, not an accumulation of techniques, proficiency in any art demands mastery of technique. Here are a few simple techniques that may help a beginning teacher.

Getting acquainted

When a beginning teacher joins a group of young children of any age, she is generally given a day to observe what is going on. While observing, there are some things she can also be doing.

Learn each child's name. Nothing so alienates a child as finding himself among people who do not know his name. Even banks, in advertising their services, put calling their depositors by name high on their list. Calling a child by his name and telling him yours is the first courtesy in beginning an acquaintance.

Learning perhaps 25 names in one morning can be aided in the following ways:

Have each child's name printed large on a 3-by-5-inch card on his back. This, incidentally, helps the children as well as the observer to recognize their names in print.

Have a list of boys' and girls' names, in age order, with space to jot down hair color, size, body build, and whatever helps you remember each of them.

Have boys' and girls names and pictures, in age order, on the bulletin board.

If a child asks your name, tell him and then ask "What's your name?" or "You're Bill, aren't you?"

Let children look you over. Before making advances toward a young child, give him time to look you over. If he likes what he sees, he may make advances to you.

Be alert to children's safety and physical well-being. The safety and physical welfare of young children come first. A good teacher never turns her back on children using equipment or tools that could lead to accidents if unsupervised. She sees that broken or splintered equipment is removed from the yard and that all climbing apparatus is steady. She also has a motherly eye for children's need for rubbers when the ground is wet, or an extra sweater when a child seems cold, or taking one off if he is getting warm.

So, even when you are observing, if a child is about to trip on untied laces, help him tie them. If a girl keeps pushing back a lock of hair from her eyes, tie the lock gently back. If a child is continually hitching a slipping shoulder strap, do your best to moor it. Doing something for a child gives both him and you the feeling that you belong where you are. You are of, with, and for the group.

Getting across

In her first days of teaching, a beginner may wonder what she should be "doing." She may even see some behavior which she feels could be influenced for the better. But how?

Teacher–child interaction may be spatial, visual, verbal, or physical. On the highway, when a traffic policeman on a motorcycle comes up alongside a car, the driver's behavior is influenced without a word being said: He draws to the side. When one child is battering or taking some equipment from another, a teacher drawing near them may encourage the battered to defend his person or property and deter his assailant from further assault—without a word being said.

In the same way, a teacher's gaze may be steadying, inquiring, encouraging, or deterring. As for gestures, the younger the child, the more likely he is to need gestures to make the meaning of words clear. He is also more in need of demonstration in such skills as putting on and off galoshes and snowpants. A demonstration of this sort is more helpful when the demonstrator sits beside rather than oposite the child, so that they are both working in the same direction. Someday watch a tennis coach demonstrate serving. He has the players stand behind him, not in front of him, to imitate his swing.

Even when physical help is given, say, to a child trying to pump herself on a swing, the help is more effective if the child is "put through" the swing's up-and-back motion by having his legs moved for him. Both putting through and showing how are more effective if what is being done is accompanied by simple statements, for example, in pulling on pants, "First one leg in, now the other leg."

This brings us to verbal interaction.

Before speaking, get a child's attention. Young children, like adults, become absorbed in what they are doing. To get in touch with a child to tell him it is time for juice, for a story, or whatever, move near him, lay a light hand on his sleeve, and say his name before whatever else is said. If he is very young, 2 or less, it may be necessary to bend down so that you are at his eye level. Calling to children across a yard or a room encourages their calling and a habit of disregarding adult voices.

The younger the child, the simpler your statement. If information of a simple sort concerning the day's routine is all that is involved in a statement, only the necessary words need be used: "Juice time now" or "Time for stories."

Act as if you expect your words to be heeded. It is said of Queen Victoria that she sat down without ever looking around, so confident was she of her loyal retainers being there with a seat of some sort. Young children, too, are influenced by the confidence in an adult's tone and action. They are suggestable, particularly around age 3, and often seem to fall in with a suggestion because they cannot, on the spur of the moment, think of a good countersuggestion.

In a university nursery school in which there had been an epidemic of dirt-throwing, I was working by my office window when I saw a student I wanted to get a message to. As I worked my way unobtrusively (I thought) round the edge of the yard, a voice said, "I'm going to throw this at you." The voice came from the ringleader of the dirt-throwers. Her arm was raised, her pan was full of dirt. With split-second calculation of the probabilities of the outcome, I said briskly, "Throw it on the ground" and kept moving toward the student with no change in pace and no backward look. The dirt was thrown on the ground.

So if you have to go out in the yard to tell a dawdler, "Time to come in for a story," don't act as if you expected to chase him around the yard to get him in. Hold out your hand with a "let's go" gesture and start moving to the door without a backward glance. You have nothing to lose in a confident bearing. Whatever happens, you will learn and that is what you are in the nursery school to do.

Give a child time to respond. You are not in the army drilling rookies. A young child's reaction time is slower than yours. If he is absorbed in what he is doing and some change in activity is shortly due, such as clearing away and washing up for lunch, give him 5 minutes' warning. "Put-away time soon, John—better begin finishing up."

Tell him what to do rather than what not to do. A child is helped by being told what to do rather than what not to do. To a boy standing in the way of a swing, say, "Over here, John. Mary's going to swing. Would you like to push her?" Not "You're on the wrong side—You're in the way of the swing"; this makes a child insecure by putting him in the wrong, without suggesting what he should do.

When in doubt do nothing, unless safety is involved. Given time, young children can solve many problems themselves. If safety is not involved and you are not sure what you should do, remember the medical axiom, "When in doubt do nothing." Just look, listen, and learn.

Developing good teacher—learner relationships

In any center for young children, a teacher learns as well as teaches; so do the children. The teacher, though, has the responsibility for creating an atmosphere in which each member can "do his thing" while respecting the rights of others to "do their thing." This calls for a few ground rules. These are made evident to the children not so much by saying as by doing what is acceptable. If children learn that what they do —with the encouragement and guidance of the teacher—leads to pleasant ongoing group activity, they come to like doing this.

How does a teacher encourage a young child to do what makes for a pleasant, mutually helpful group?

Approve the deed, as well as or rather than, the doer. Very young children have difficulty in separating the deed from the doer. They can be helped by having praise attached to deeds rather than doers. In place of "good boy" or "good," try "Thank you for bringing me the book," with a rewarding smile. Or, to the child who has consoled a fallen comrade, an approving, "You are helping him to feel better"; or "How clean you've wiped the table" or "What a good job you did in stacking the blocks."

Here is an illustration of how misleading a word of commendation may be if it is not attached to what it commends. In a nursery school in which I looked at the children's throats as they entered the nursery school in the morning, I fell into the habit of saying a smiling "good," as I patted each child on the back after looking into his open mouth. This rite apparently impressed the children as a therapeutic procedure. About this time, a 2-year-old's father developed a serious throat infection. Without the antibiotics of today, the family doctor, a consultant, and the little boy's mother became more grave each time the father's throat was looked at. Seeing this unsatisfactory state of affairs in which looking at a throat was only leading to head-shaking and anxiety, the little boy said, "If Miss Landreth were to look at him, he would say "ah," and she would say 'good.'"

Redirect unacceptable activity in line with what a child is seeking. What a child does represents his notion of how to deal with a problem. If such dealing is unacceptable, what he needs is an acceptable way of achieving what he wants. If a 3-year-old begins throwing sand in the sandbox, consider possible reasons. Has he been sitting quietly in the sand for a long time? May he now feel the need for activity? Suggest, "Get yourself a ball, Bill, if you want to throw." If his throwing sand seems an attempt to attract another child's attention, offer a technique better calculated to make friends: "Ask Jim if he would like to dig with you. Tell him he could make a hole too." If the sand-throwing seems to be in protest against crowding and interference from too many children trying to use the sandbox, suggest another activity for the last-comers, explaining they can come back later when there is room.

Try to foresee and forestall trouble. If you are alert to what is going on, you can often forestall trouble with a timely suggestion. Suppose you have some children gathered closely around you for a story and a rambunctious boy who likes a front seat is running to join you. Don't wait for him to elbow his way in. Ask the children to move back a bit and say in a welcoming tone, "Here's a place for you Bill," pointing to a place for him to sit.

Put it their way. Two- and three-year-olds come to a center to play, not to improve their cognition or their characters. Their play is often make-believe activity. Fit in with it. To a captain on a rocking boat who is not heeding the protests of passengers who want off, try, "Captain, some passengers want off —better slow the boat." To a child who puts an arm in front of you with a playful "You can't pass," put your hand in an imaginary pocket and, with a handing-over gesture, say "Here's my pass."

Set a good example. Children learn from what you do as well as what you say. In a university nursery school, there was a rule that the slide to the tree house could be climbed up or slid down—never run down. One morning, when most of the children had left for home, a student teacher in a moment of youthful abandon, ran down, slipped, fell, and broke her arm. The few children around could hardly believe what they saw. "She ran down the slide," they told each other, big-eyed. During the weeks she was in school with the cast, they pointed her out to parents and visitors, explaining the nature of her misdeed and its dire consequences.

Safe use of equipment is not the only behavior in which a teacher sets an example. Acceptance of food served at lunch or snack time is another. So is her way of interacting with children. For this reason she avoids issues that lead to contention rather than cooperation or constructive learning. When four or five 3-year-olds come to a clay table, one of them may attempt to corner as much clay as possible. "You must not take more clay" or "You have all you need" invites defiance and directs children's attention to how little or how much each of them have. Since the clay is there to be made into something, why not ask, "What are you going to make with the clay?" thereby directing attention to manipulation rather than accumulation. As making gets underway, the teacher can unobtrusively reapportion the clay.

Help children modify unacceptable expressions of feelings, but acknowledge the reality of feelings—yours as well as theirs. When a group of people of any age get together day in and day out, there will be periods of disaffection.

There was once a nursery school convention of countering a child's heated "I don't like you" with a pious "I like you." This suggested that it was both possible and desirable to like everyone all the time. Is it?

Recently I attended a case presentation at a children's behavior clinic. When the psychiatrist, the psychologist, and the psychiatric social worker had completed their reports on a child who obviously presented a most difficult problem, the director of the institute asked the psychiatrist if he would handle the case any differently if he had a chance to repeat his efforts. The psychiatrist thought a moment before replying that, if he were doing it again, he would limit the therapy sessions to 20 minutes, as it was difficult to "like" the child for more than 20 minutes at a time.

A teacher's acceptance of feelings is often better expressed in what she does not say than what she says. Bob, aged 3.10, was given to direct personal attacks when he was in any way crossed by his mother. He had also played a good deal with older boys who were amused by his childish rages when they frustrated or teased him. He blossomed in the nursery school environment, with its relative lack of frustrating situations and the consistent methods of procedure. One noon when he had dawdled throughout his meal, despite the teacher's warning that lunch would be over soon, he was too late to get his dessert—which happened to be one of his favorites; he went to the bathroom to get ready to go home without it. He was very angry. As the teacher followed him to the bathroom, he looked at her with red face and quivering lip and said, "I'd like to put you in the toilet and then flush it!" The teacher said nothing for a few minutes. She realized that Bob was exercising commendable restraint in merely disposing of her verbally. Appreciating both his feelings and his progress in modifying his response to them, she said quietly, "Bob, you took so long to eat your meat and vegetables today, lunch was over before you got to dessert. Tomorrow, keep eating and you'll have plenty of time to finish lunch and dessert."

All of these interactions are ones in which a child can learn something about getting along with other people. Other teacher–child interactions help a child learn how to learn, observe, compare, relate, speculate, and persevere.

Developing helpful learning habits

"Make your habits your friends" is stitched on an old New England sampler. Some teacher–learner interactions help such habits develop.

Let a child do all that he is able. A young child perfects his ripening skills through guided practice. Such practice makes a child confident and independent as well as more expert. Because young children are laboratory, rather than lecture, students, they use a lot of materials that have to be prepared and put out for them. If a teacher does the preparing, time spent in preparation is time spent away from the children. If the children themselves do it, they learn as they do.

Take the preparation of brush paints: A child as young as 3 years of age can prepare these if the paint jars have two clearly marked rings—one for the amount of powder or paste, the other for the amount of water to add—and a tongue depressor for mixing each jar. This calls also for running water and a workbench at child height, for labeled paint shelves, and for color strips as well as printed labels on the cans or cartons of paint powder. But think what a child can learn not only in measuring and mixing but in associating printed words with colors. A pictured mixing-direction chart with a left–right order gives practice in reading (picture) directions.

When a painting is finished and a child asks for his name to be printed, why not show him how to add at least his initials before he hangs his painting on a drying line? Washing brushes and jars and wiping an easel is pure pleasure for a child who likes the feel and look of water. And what child does not? A helper's waterproof apron donned for such activities is a symbol of responsibility as well as protection for clothes.

With ingenuity, patience, and planning, a teacher can develop a core of teaching aides from her 2-, 3-, and 4-year-old learners.

Delay giving help until a child seems ready for it. Timing of help is important. Letting a child struggle unsuccessfully with a problem to the point of tearful frustration may make him less eager and confident in attacking problems later.

To a child wrenching on a wagon jammed into a tree trunk, a teacher might try, "What seems to be the matter? Let's take a look. Could we try lifting it like this?"

Let a child experience success. Children need to experience success in order to persevere for it. Navajo Indians, in training children to hunt, often put small animals in the traps so that young hunters can experience success. A teacher can give a young child the same experience when, after difficulties and some help from her, he fastens the last button, zips up the last inch, puts in the last piece of a puzzle, hammers in the last nail on a box.

Ask, don't tell, a child anything that he can see for himself. Some of the learning problems a child is faced with are of seeing rather than doing. When a guinea pig is brought into a child's group following some visits of a rabbit and a mouse, should no comment be forthcoming from the children, a question, "Does the guinea pig have a tail?" may lead to observation and comparison that might not otherwise have occurred. Asking such questions suggests that a child can find out for himself by looking, listening, and handling, rather than always asking an adult.

Suggest, don't state, possible solutions. In thinking about and trying to solve problems, a child has to draw on hunches and consider more than one possibility. One way of helping a child to consider possibilities is to offer suggestions. To a child overbalanced on the teeter-totter, "You could try moving further from the pivot," involves a child's thinking more than a flat "Move further from the pivot." Suggestions of a "you could," "you might," and "let us" type have a take-or-leave-it quality. They also suggest that a child can and should think through problems himself. For this reason, a teacher has to be clear on when it is appropriate to offer a child a choice.

Be clear on whether you are offering a child a choice. When you ask "Would you like to come now for juice?" you are offering a choice and must be prepared to accept "no" or "yes." If you do not wish to offer a choice, "Juice time now," makes this clear.

So, also, "toilet now," lifts the responsibility for decision from a restless 2-year-old who has not yet learned to make this decision. Once he has learned to make it, "Do you need to go to the toilet?" reminds him to make the choice himself.

If reasons are given for requests, they should be logical. Recently I watched some children watering the beds around a nursery school yard. Turns with the two watering cans were eagerly sought. When the beds were fairly awash, two boys who had been waiting in line were happily filling their cans when a student teacher approached. "Let's put the cans away, you've had enough watering," she said. In outraged frustration, the boys flung their cans on the ground. It was the beds, not the boys, that had enough watering. For that matter, who but a 3-year-old boy knows when he has had *enough* watering?

When logical reasons are given for requests, children learn to look for causal relationships. For this reason, "We don't spit" is open to question because some do. "If you want to spit, spit in the toilet—spitting dirties the floor," avoids misstatement and, incidentally, takes most of the charm from spitting.

Ask or tell in words that a young child understands. A mother whose 3-year-old son was reluctant to have her leave him in nursery school told him she would be back at 11:00 when the hands on her watch had gone to where she pointed. She had barely left when the child started asking the teachers if it were now 11:00 and would they show him where the hands were on their watches. The head teacher explained, "Your mother will come back after you have had juice and a story. Let us go in now and get the juice ready." With the duration of his mother's absence thus brought within his comprehension, the child relaxed and, sure enough, at the end of the story his mother appeared.

"Information" does not inform unless it is related to a young child's experience and way of thinking.

Analyzing
teacher—learner interaction

How a teacher interacts with a child in getting acquainted with him, getting across to him, developing a good teacher–learner relationship and good learning habits is the basis of her individual teaching style. No two teachers will be quite the same. But all beginning teachers can profit from some analysis of the effectiveness of their interactions. Analyses, to be helpful, should be based on a verbatim written record of (1) what a child said or did, at what time of day, in what setting that prompted the teacher–child interaction; (2) what the teacher said and did; and (3) what the child said or did in response.

USING EDUCATIONAL STRATEGIES
SELECTIVELY AND ADAPTIVELY

Teacher–child interaction is affected by the educational strategies a teacher uses. What is an educational strategy?

I recently visited a research center in which disadvantaged 5-year-olds were being taught to read by a teaching machine. To get to the observation booth, visitors passed through a room with a large electronic computer complex with lights flashing, machinery clicking, and two computer attendants attending. In the darkened soundproof booth, the tour conductor drew our attention to what could be seen through the one-way observation mirror—four cubicles, each with a television screen, headphones, and an electric pointer. As we looked, an adult came in with four children. Each of them went to a cubicle, put on the headphones, and picked up the pointer.

"Half a million dollars' worth of hardware here," the tour conductor said proudly. On contact, the hardware began instructing each child through his headphones to point to one of two words that went with a picture, for example, *boy* and *box*. When the child pointed to the right word, a drawing of a smiling face flashed on the screen. When he pointed to the wrong one, a dejected face appeared.

"The machine is reinforcing them," the tour conductor explained. "Only an affluent society," an English visitor murmured, "could afford to spend half a million dollars to teach 5-year-olds the difference between *boy* and *box*."

"That child seems to be doing a lot of fidgeting and looking around," said a first-grade teacher in the tour group.

"But she's not bothering anyone, like she would in a class," countered the tour operator.

During the half hour the children spent in the cubicles, the adult with them appeared to be functioning as an attendant, keeping machine–child interaction going.

This is an educational strategy in which a machine does the teaching it has been programmed to do and another machine in another room records each child's successes and failures so they can be analyzed later. This hardware strategy had a simpler beginning.

Educational play materials and equipment

The strategy began with Montessori educational equipment. Madam Maria Montessori was an Italian physician and educator who undertook, at the beginning of the century, the education of what would now be called "educationally disadvantaged children" in a large housing complex in Rome. Believing that young children learn through sensing and perceiving, she designed teaching materials that rivet attention on differences in size, shape, color, tone, and texture. Among the simpler of the great variety of materials so ingeniously devised by her are:

Form boards with insets of different sizes and shapes that can be fitted in only when a child matches the size and shape of the inset to the size and shape of the space it fits.

Blocks of graded length that make a stair only when arranged in length order.

Color samples, tuned metal bells, and textile fragments of coarse and smooth textures. Two sets of these can be paired only by paying attention to color, tone, and texture.

Each piece sets a problem and each rewards the child by making his success apparent. For this reason, staff members in Montessori schools were originally not called "teachers." They functioned as "supervisors," who saw that the equipment was used only as Montessori intended. The equipment did the teaching. Modern Montessori schools have somewhat modified the teacher's role, but the use of Montessori equipment is still central.

Today, educational or creative play materials are a billion-dollar industry that brings educational materials into many homes as well as schools. Such educational materials or tools range in sophistication from nested hollow blocks, which a 2-year-old can nest only when they are put together in size order, to Cuisenaire rods that can be used in arithmetic problems. These consist of 10 rods, each a different color, which represent a 1-to-10 range in length. In using them a child can discover the combination of rod lengths that equals a 10-length rod.

A much more complex educational tool is the electric talking typewriter, which was developed to teach young children to read, type, and compose stories. To briefly describe its use, a 3-year-old goes into a booth where he finds an electric typewriter with a screen above it. He taps a key, the letter appears on the screen, and a voice names it. After some experience of this sort with whatever key he taps, he finds on a later encounter that only one key produces a letter and its sound. This makes him look closely at the key letter to see what makes it different. Once he has learned it, other letters are added in the same way. The "aha, that's it" thrill of achievement keeps him going: keeps him paying attention and doing what is needed to learn.

Assets of these tools, machines, or play materials are that they induce a child to learn at his own rate and reward him with the satisfaction of achievement. They are, therefore, excellent supplements to any teaching process, though all are expensive, and the talking typewriter is exhorbitantly so. Since hardware tends to be overvalued in our computerized technocracy, some shortcomings of these educational tools should be kept in mind. The tasks most set are repetitions of a process that a child no longer needs once he has learned the process. But to justify their cost, they are sometimes used long after they serve any learning purpose for a particular child. Further, as most educational play materials set a specific problem, they do not challenge a child to set his own. And, of course, equipment alone cannot provide an integrated learning program without skilled learner–teacher interaction. Even so, a glance at a play material catalog, such as *Creative Playthings*, offers an impressive review of many of the basic learning problems of young children. *It also suggests ways of using inexpensive household supplies to achieve some of the same purposes.*

Educational games
(often thinly disguised drills)

Just as educational play materials owe much to Montessori, so do educational games owe a debt to Friedrich Froebel. He was a German philosopher and educator of the eighteenth century, who is generally regarded as the father of the kindergarten. He held mystical beliefs about innate ideas in young children that could be developed through use of the "gifts" (balls and cubes) and the "games" he devised. To illustrate, he suggested that, in using his eight cubes, a nurse sing to her 3-year-old charge:

> *Look here and see!*
> *One whole, two halves;*
> *One half, two-fourths;*
> *two halves, four-fourths;*
> *One whole, four-fourths;*
> *Four fourths, eight eights;*
> *Eight eights, one whole.*
> *Here are many, here are few;*
> *It's a magic way to do.*

Today, the content of games is planned to help a child develop language and concepts of number, color, position, and the like. Finger plays, such as "Ten little blackbirds sitting on a hill," sing about the numbers 1 to 10 with some action accompaniment. "I put my right hand in, I put my right hand out," emphasizes knowing right from left. Variations of "Simon says" and "If you're happy, clap your hands" sing about moving or pointing to body parts. Regardless of content, these games all have an aura of the kindergarten at the turn of the century, with the teacher at the center and a great deal of singing or saying in unison.

They still, though, have their advocates. A much publicized

project for disadvantaged 5-year-olds at the University of
Illinois drills young children in the use of language with a lot
of shouting and handclapping. In a drill on "not statements"
a teacher is told to:

a. Point to a child and ask a question that can be answered with
   yes. "Is this a boy?"
b. Nod your head in an exaggerated fashion and say, "Yes. This is
   a boy."
c. Point to a girl and ask the original question, "Is this a boy?"
d. Shake your head vigorously, "No. This is not a boy." Accent the
   word with a clap.
Repeat this procedure with other familiar objects [*everyone shouting and clapping together*].[3]

Such games, in small doses, adapted or spontaneously in-
vented to help a learning process, can be a useful supplement
in a child's learning numbers, letters, directions, or other bits
of information. Advertising agencies would not set such store
by singing commercials if their captive audiences did not
learn something from them. But, as an educational curriculum
with enforced participation by all children, regardless of their
needs or interests, educational games could turn young children off games and gamesy teachers forever.

Here, though, is an imaginative variation of the game
strategy in which a kindergarten teacher made a playful approach to stimulating children's thinking about the function of
color in nature: Fall berries brought in by one of the children
for "show and tell" led to talk about finding berries. "Let's
play a game," said the teacher. "Here is a packet of plain
toothpicks, here is one of red picks. Who would like to scatter
them in the playyard? Let's pretend that the scattered picks
are berries and that we are hungry birds and see how many
berries we can find in 5 minutes." The "birds" were off in a

[3]Carl Bereiter and Siegfried Engelmann, *Teaching disadvantaged children in the preschool* (Englewood Cliffs, N.J.: Prentice-Hall, 1966),
p. 143.

flash, and at the end of 5 minutes, two piles of berries were back on the classroom table—one much bigger than the other. Which berries are easier for birds to find and why was only one of the gains of the game. It led later to what is hard to find (animals and plants the same color as their background) and to the use of camouflage.

Educationally productive play

For 40 years, free (presumably educationally productive) play has been the educational hallmark of the nursery school. It has the advantage of giving each child a chance to choose activities he is interested in and to pursue them at his own level of functioning. An excellent early example of educationally productive play is described by an English psychologist, Susan Isaacs, in her account of her school for the young children of Cambridge dons (professors).

A scientist herself, she treated her child companions—the children of scholars and scientists—like amateur scientists, just as Tolstoy treated his peasant pupils like amateur writers. They learned from their own experience, with a variety of simple materials—wood ends, clay, water, metals, yarns, paper, and such tools as saws, hammers, and scissors. They also learned from their excursions around Cambridge, which were always planned with a specific purpose, such as to find out how ladders were made at a time when the children had difficulty making a satisfactory ladder themselves. All the time, the children kept up a continuing dialogue with each other and with Susan Isaacs about what they thought and did. The general atmosphere, with its child-initiated projects or experiments and ongoing discussion, deduction, and induction, was not unlike that of a Cambridge laboratory.

To what lengths Susan Isaacs went to let the children learn from their own experience, to guess about what they did not know and then test their guess, is illustrated in what happened when the school rabbit died. The day after its burial, the children speculated on its possible afterlife. Had the rabbit gone to heaven—fur, claws, whiskers, and all? How could they find out? Susan Isaacs did not deter her young empiricists from exploratory disinterment.

The best of today's English infant rooms try to carry on the Susan Isaacs tradition. So do many university nursery schools in the United States. At its best, educationally productive play is the most exciting strategy for both children and teachers, who become as one in such a venture. It makes, though, the most exacting demands on a teacher for breadth of knowledge and interests as well as for understanding young learners. Since young children are learning all the time, a teacher has to be so "programmed" that she can, on the spur of the moment, develop the educational content of any activity or experience in a way that does not rob the child of discovery. So, it is perhaps not surprising that free play is often not as educationally productive as it might be, or that it often seems to lack from–to learning progression, or that the educational content of many an experience is overlooked.

Some years ago, a graduate student who was working in a nursery school said to me, "I think one of the boys is a bit curious about gravity. The other day when a plane went over he said to me, 'Why can't you move through the air?' " "You know," the student said, "I couldn't think what to tell him."

Actually, he didn't have to tell him anything about "gravity." He could have made a standing jump and said, "*I can* move through the air." That boy, 4-year-old son of a Nobel scientist, was observant enough to have said, "But you can't move very far." Even if he hadn't said this, the student could have gone on to say, "I can move farther when I get up more force." And with this, he could have run vigorously into a broad jump. Even if this left him breathless and the child speechless, he could still, I think, have assumed that he had given the child at least a glimmer of the notion that, in order for something to move through the air, one force—gravity—must be overcome by another force. This is something that a nursery school child has already experienced. The harder he throws something up in the air, the farther it goes, and the longer it takes to come down.[4]

Despite a few missed opportunities of this sort, an educationally productive play environment that encourages young children to be curious, to ask questions, speculate, and then test their speculations does develop the spirit and process of scientific inquiry.

In a university nursery school, a 3-year-old ran up to another boy at the carpentry bench. "I have proof," he said. "There is a bottom to the sandbox." The carpenter ran back with him to the sandbox, where the young empiricist clinched what had apparently been an argument by pointing to his excavation leading to the solid cement bottom of the sandbox. To the exhilaration of discovery was added the confidence that came of knowing why he knew what he did. He had proof—the yardstick of validity.

Educational projects

One way of ensuring some progression and continuity in children's learning, as well as substantial content, is through collaborating with them in a project of particular interest to them. Using their interest as a starting point, a teacher can help them develop a sequence of experiences rich in related concepts and skills.

This strategy owes something to John Dewey, an American philosopher and educator of the twentieth and late nineteenth centuries, who suggested that what a child is taught should be presented in such a way that he sees its purpose and usefulness. Teachers interpreted his educational philosophy as meaning don't drill a child in such skills as adding, subtracting, and multiplying; instead, have arithmetic processes of this sort learned incidentally in playing store. This project strategy

---

[4]Catherine Landreth, *Early childhood: behavior and learning* (New York Knopf, 1967), p. 275.

was particularly popular in progressive schools, and it still has its merits, particularly for 4- and 5-year-olds.

Consider what a child *could* learn through his interest in sending and getting something through the mail about the postal system; about specialized occupational contributions to society; about dates, addresses, and geographical locations; and about printing, counting, and measuring time and weight. What he *would* learn from a project like this would depend on how much he was encouraged to do and find out himself. An educational project is not a show-and-tell presentation by a teacher.

This, though, brings us to a fifth strategy in which the entire emphasis is on show and tell.

Educational exposure
(show-and-tell television educational programs)

Since "Sesame Street" went on the air, dramatically acclaimed as a "wall-less, nationwide nursery school," and solidly subsidized by federal and foundation funds, no account of educational strategies for stimulating learning in young children would be complete without reference to educational television. Television, as Marshall McLuhan reminds us, is only an extension and expansion of what a young child can see and hear in his daily exposure to the life around him. What can it do?

What it *can't* do is give a young child an opportunity to learn from his own firsthand experience, to generalize in his own words, and to apply and test what he has learned in a somewhat different situation. Instead, a child is a passive viewer and listener. He is told and shown. What he learns from this, presumably, is, that the way a young child learns is by being told and shown. Nothing could be farther from the findings of 50 years of research on how infants and young children learn.

Something else a television program cannot do is provide ongoing interaction between teacher and learner. A television screen cannot respond to a young child's question or puzzled look. Because it cannot, there is no guarantee that what a producer thinks he is putting into a performance is what a young child will get out of it. Years ago, the playwright James Barrie, wishing to get children's reaction's to a new production of Peter Pan, reserved a box for some of his young friends for the opening performance. When it was over, he joined the children and asked, "What did you like best?" "What we liked best," they told him with sparkling eyes, "was tearing up the program and dropping the bits on people's heads in the stalls."

What television *can* do is clearest in its commercials. It can rivet attention on an idea or piece of propaganda through a variety of visual and auditory attention-grabbers. Its jingles stick in the mind. But is this sticking-in-the-mind learning?

A mother whose children had grown up returned after a lapse of several years to teaching first grade. During her first week she tried to stimulate rapport and conversation by asking the children to tell the group something interesting that had happened at home. "Interesting," to the children, apparently meant "unusual." They vied with each other in reports of how mother fell off the stepladder, the dog got run over in the drive, and father cut himself with the power saw and had to have stitches. Discouraged by these accounts of domestic carnage, the teacher changed the conversational topic for the second week. "Today," she said, "I'd like you to tell me a happy thought." There was a long silence. Then a little girl stood up, "I think I'm pregnant," she said. As this remark held no possibilities for conversational expansion, the teacher let it pass with a quiet "Thank you." It stayed in her mind, though, and that night she called the little girl's mother who greeted her account with a gale of laughter. At breakfast that morning as she was shaking the crispies into the children's bowls, she had said to her husband, "I think I'm pregnant." "That's a happy thought," he muttered.[5]

"Sesame Street" jingles are about the letters of the alphabet; the numbers to 10 in serial order; sizes, shapes, posi-

[5]*Ibid.*, pp. 202–203.

tions, directions; and such concepts as *same* and *different*—all
of which seem basic to thinking processes. These, though, are
generally presented out of any natural context in which a
young child might see their purpose and usefulness in his own
life. But then it is difficult to tell for what age group this program is intended. In one sequence in which a muppet cries
because he is told he will have to go into the hospital to get
his tonsils out, Gordon (an adult) speaks of his own "personal
experience" and "honest apprehension" about this "minor
operation."

Could an educational television program for young children
do better? Could it take advantage of its unique medium to
offer visual and aural experiences that would bring the won-
ders of a child's world within the grasp of his mind?

One reason for promoting educational television programs
for young children is to make up for possible lacks in the
lives of poor children who are not too poor to lack access to
a television set. One of their lacks is sufficient friendly, encouraging contact with a familiar understanding adult.
Though a face on the screen may not be the same as a face
that smiles back at you, a screen face may be better than an
absent one. "Sesame Street" makes no attempt to provide this
kind of personal intimacy. It is "show biz," with fast-paced
vaudeville action and interaction among adults, muppets, and
animated cartoons. When children appear on the program,
neither the children nor the adults seem comfortable in each
other's presence.

In pleasant contrast is a program called "Play School"
(Australian Broadcasting Company) for 3- and 4-year-olds.
It opens with an attractive young man and woman, getting
ready for their half-hour program, who look up and smile
with a friendly hello, as the camera pans in on them through
the open door of the play school. This is not show biz. It is as
low-keyed, friendly, and natural as dropping in on a child's

favorite uncle or aunt. These young people, with no supporting muppets or animated cartoons, seem happily at home with young children. Everything they do, say, or sing is directed to their invisible audience of 3- and 4-year-olds, each of whom might well feel that everything is just for him. A story—told, not read—in which the storyteller became each of several rather dim-witted animals but remained "on to" 3- and 4-year-olds' superiority to such foolishness, suggests what an asset a good storyteller could be in any program for young children.

Something else a television program could do is give young children ideas for inventive use of the kinds of material that are around most homes—paper bags, paper plates, cans, plastic jars, bottle tops, bits of string and yarn. Young children love to make things. Making things can lead to measuring, counting, drawing, planning, and using such simple tools as blunt-tipped kindergarten scissors, paper staplers, and punches.

Young children are also eager cooks. A junior Julia Child-type session could show them how to boil eggs, and to make custard, ice cream, and even bread. Cooking introduces measurement of time, temperature, and volume, as well as reading pictograph recipes and seeing how heat and cold change solids and liquids.

Because television is not limited by space and time, it is an ideal medium for giving glimpses of what a young child might otherwise not see, such as a father's day at work. And, because inner-city children may know *water* only as something that comes from a tap and goes down a drain, something poured in a glass, or run in a bath, what a scenario could be based on water! Television can not only bring a mountain to a moppet, it can also put together the glimpses of a larger world than his home in such a way that a child can put together what he knows. He can see for himself what is the same and what is different without such "Sesame Street" statements as "Racoons' claws are like hands. They have the *same kind of flexibility.*"

A statement often made about "Sesame Street" is that it costs $8 million to produce. The educational value of a television program cannot be gauged by what is spent on it. This is also true of the other four strategies that require use of educational play materials, games, projects, and play. They are not ends in themselves. They are means by which the nature of a childs' world and his relationship to it is brought within the grasp of his mind at successive stages in his growth of understanding. Their effective use lies in selecting and adapting the strategy best suited to a particular child for a particular learning process.

FOR
FURTHER READING

PRESCHOOL CHILDREN: EACH DIFFERENT

Landreth, C. *Early childhood: behavior and learning.* New York: Knopf, 1967. This textbook offers a review, evaluation, and some applications of the research on which this book is based.

Scrimshaw, N. S. "Infant malnutrition and adult learning." *Saturday Review*, 84 (1968): 64–66. This is a brief report on the relationships found between malnutrition and adult learning by one of the leading investigators.

WHAT MAKES THEM LEARN?

Dawe, H. C. "A study of the effect of an educational program upon language development and related mental functions in young children." *Journal of Experimental Education* 11(1942): 200–209. This is one of the earliest studies demonstrating effective ways of enriching an educationally restricted (orphanage) environment.

Dennis, W., and Sayegh, Y. "The effects of supplementary experiences upon the behavioral development of infants in institutions." *Child Development* 36(1965): 81–90. This article relates differences in infant development to differences in their experiences.

Holt, J. *How children learn.* New York: Pitman, 1969. Full of incidents of an infant or young child learning on his own.

Jensen, A. R. "Learning in the preschool years." *Journal of Nursery Education* 18(1963): 133–139. This article describes experiments on the effects of labeling on learning.

Piaget, J., and Inhelder, B. *The psychology of the child.* Translated by H. Weaver. New York: Basic Books, 1969.

WHAT CAN THEY LEARN?

San Francisco Unified School District. *A curriculum guide for children's centers and prekindergarten.* 1969. This is a three-column outline of learning sequences in 10 related areas of learning, the purposes of each sequence, and suggested teaching devices for promoting each of them, along with some illustrative learning experiences and learning assessment items. Also suggested are a daily activity plan and guides to safety measures, health education, nutrition education, nap and bathroom procedures, and effective management of field trips and excursions.

Dewey, J. *The child and the curriculum.* Chicago: University of Chicago Press, 1902. "Relevance" in a curriculum for children at the turn of the century is discussed.

FROM BABBLING TO LANGUAGE

Chukovsky, K. *From two to five.* Translated by M. Morton. Berkeley: University of California Press, 1963. The young child's creative approach to acquiring his mother tongue is described.

Irwin, O. C. "Infant speech: effect of systematic reading of stories." *Journal of Speech and Hearing Research* 3(1960): 187–190. Evidence of infant speech stimulation resulting from being read stories from 13 to 30 months of age is presented.

Weir, R. *Language in the crib.* The Hague: Mouton, 1962. The bedtime soliloquies (taped by his mother) of a child under 30 months of age reveal his self-imposed speech practice.

FROM DECODING GRAPHIC SYMBOLS TO READING

Ashton-Warner, S. *Teacher.* New York: Simon & Schuster, 1963. Some suggestions for stimulating interest in beginning reading are given.

Durkin, D. *Children who read early.* New York: Teachers College, 1966. The behavior and environment characteristics of some early readers are analyzed.

Frost, J. L. (ed.). *Issues and innovations in the teaching of reading.* Glenview, Ill.: Scott, Foresman, 1967. This is a competent review by several reading specialists.

FROM EXPERIENCING TO PROCESSING INFORMATION

Medawar, P. B. *The art of the soluble.* London: Methuen, 1967. This is a lucid and witty discussion of scientific thinking by a British Nobel Prize winner.

FROM MAGIC TO NATURAL PHENOMENA

Piaget, J. "The child and modern physics." *Scientific American* 196(1957): 46–51. Piaget compares infants' and young children's conclusions about the nature of the physical world with those of scientists.

Science Curriculum Improvement Study. *Material objects: teachers' guide.* Preliminary edition. Berkeley: University of California, 1966. A variety of sorting activities that make children aware of objects and their properties and of seriating objects is suggested.

FROM LINES, DAUBS, AND SMEARS TO PICTURES

Kellogg, R., with O'Dell, S. *The psychology of children's art.* New York: C.R.M. Random House, 1967. Common features in the paintings of young children, based on an extensive worldwide collection, are analyzed.

Johnson, H. M. *The art of block building.* New York: Day, 1933. This text offers many sketches of young children's block constructions. Although it is now out of print, it is still available in many libraries.

FROM BOUNCING TO DANCING

Building childrens personalities with creative dancing. 30 min, 16mm, sound, color. Frank Goldsmith Productions, Educational Film Series, University of California Extension Media, Los Angeles, 1954. This film shows a teacher in an outdoor class skillfully guiding and encouraging each child toward a unique personal style.

FROM "ME" TO "WHO AM I?"

Aries, P. *Centuries of childhood.* New York: Knopf, 1962. Attitudes toward children throughout different centuries, in some of which childhood was not recognized as a separate state, are contrasted.

Bronfenbrenner, V. *Two worlds of childhood: U.S. and U.S.S.R.* New York: Russell Sage, 1970. The pervasive influence of social philosophy on education and the rearing of young children in Russia is analyzed and contrasted with education and child rearing in the United States.

Erikson, E. E. *Childhood and society.* New York: Norton, 1950; Chapter 7. Eight stages of man suggest eight stages in ego (who am I?) development.

Ewald, C. *My little boy.* Translated by A. T. De Mattos. New York: Scribner, 1906. An unusually perceptive father writes, with Hans Christian Andersen charm, of his little boy's discovery of himself and his world. This text is out of print but available in most libraries.

TEACHING: WHAT IS IT?

Bereiter, C., and Engelman, S. *Teaching disadvantaged children in the preschool.* Englewood Cliffs, N.J.: Prentice-Hall, 1966. An educational strategy that relies mainly on verbal drills is described.

Featherstone, J. "The primary school revolution in Britain." Originally this article appeared as three articles in *The New Republic*, 1967 (August 10, September 2, and September 9). This reprint describes the experiences offered children in the English infant schools (for children 5–7 years of age).

Froebel, F. W. A. *Pedagogics of the kindergarten*. New York: Appleton, 1909. Translated by J. Jarvis. Froebel's ideas concerning the play and playthings of the young child are given.

Gray, S. R., and Klaus, R. A. "An experimental preschool program for culturally deprived children." *Child Development* 36(1965): 887–898. The program, purposes, and results of an educational experiment with young children and their parents in Tennessee are described.

Isaacs, S. "The experimental construction of an environment optimal for mental growth." In *A handbook of child psychology*, edited by C. Murchinson. Worcester, Mass.: Clark University, 1931. A description of what went on in Dr. Susan Isaacs's school for the young children of Cambridge University scholars and scientists.

Montessori, M. *The Montessori method*. Translated by A. E. George. New York: Schocken Books, 1965. This is the basic text on Montessori methods and materials.

Pines, M. *Revolution in learning*. New York: Harper & Row, 1966. An overview of some educational experiments in early childhood learning from 1960 to 1966 is presented by a journalist.

Richardson, E. S. *In the early world*. Wellington, New Zealand: Whitcombe & Tombs, 1964. This is a description, with beautiful illustrations, of what went on in a small country school for New Zealand Maori and pakeha (European origin) children who developed into amateur naturalists, artists, and craftsmen while their teacher developed along with them.

Tolstoy, L. *Tolstoy on education*. This is a translation by L. Weiner, of Tolstoy's *Pedagogical articles 1862*. Chicago: University of Chicago Press, 1967. Tolstoy's school for peasant children at Yásnaya Polyána is described.

PROFESSIONAL JOURNALS

Childhood Education. Journal of the Association for Childhood Education International, 3615 Wisconsin Avenue, N.W., Washington, D.C. 20016.

Children. Published by the Office of Child Development, Children's Bureau, P.O. Box 1182, Washington, D.C. 20013.

Young Children. Journal of the National Association for Education of Young Children, 1834 Connecticut Avenue, N.W., Washington, D.C. 20009.

INDEX